D0291333

37653006003407
Main NonFiction: 5th floor
551.65 LOFFMAN
The traveler's weather
guide

APR 9 7

CENTRAL ARKANSAS
LIBRARY SYSTEM
LITTLE ROCK PUBLIC LIBRARY
700 LOUISIANA
LITTLE ROCK, ARKANSAS

DEMCO

The Traveler's Weather Guide

by Tom Loffman

Ten Speed Press
Berkeley, California

Copyright © 1996 by Tom Loffman

All rights reserved. No part of this book may be reproduced in any form, except brief excerpts for the purpose of review, without the written permission of the publisher.

Ten Speed Press
P.O. Box 7123
Berkeley, California 94707

A Kirsty Melville Book

Distributed in Australia by E.J. Dwyer Pty. Ltd., in Canada by Publishers Group West, in New Zealand by Tandem Press, in South Africa by Real Books, in the United Kingdom and Europe by Airlift Books, and in Singapore and Malaysia by Berkeley Books.

Cover design by Design Site
Cover photography by Tom Loffman
Interior design and composition by Jeff Brandenburg, ImageComp

Library of Congress Cataloging-in-Publication Data

Loffman, Tom.
        The traveler's weather guide / by Tom Loffman.
            p.   cm.
        Includes index.
        ISBN 0-89815-831-1 (paper)
        1. Weather. 2. Climatology. I. Title.
        QC981.L65   1996
        551.6—dc20   96-11785
                                                                CIP

Printed in Canada

Weather Records

Comparative Climatic Data: *National Climatic Data Center, Asheville, N.C.*

Tables of Temperature, Relative Humidity, and Precipitation for the World: *World Climatology Branch of the Meteorological Office, London, England*

Worldwide Airfield Summaries: *USAF (ETAC) Washington, D.C.*

Weather Records: *National Climatic Data Center, Asheville, N. Carolina*

1 2 3 4 5 6 — 00 99 98 97 96

CENTRAL ARKANSAS LIBRARY SYSTEM
LITTLE ROCK PUBLIC LIBRARY
700 LOUISIANA STREET
LITTLE ROCK, AR 72201

Table of Contents

Introduction

When you're traveling, whether it's a vacation or a business trip, there's no doubt about it—if the weather is bad, you're going to be miserable. And you're going to be even more unhappy when you figure out how much money the whole thing cost you. Even if the weather isn't horrible, it can be wet or cold, and that means you have to lug around extra clothing and coverups. Who needs the aggravation?

And yet, every day, there are tens of thousands (or perhaps even millions) of unhappy travelers who found out too late that they should have been here last (or next) month. For every location on Earth there's a time when the weather is at its best—and a time when it's at its worst. The trick is to find out about the weather *before* you make your reservations.

Complete, reliable, easy-to-understand weather information for worldwide travel planning has been hard to find, and has never been gathered together in one convenient package—at least, not until now. *The Traveler's Weather Guide* was researched and written with the traveler specifically in mind.

This book isn't just a collection of numbers. It's designed so that you can easily locate your destination in the tables, and quickly plan your trip around the weather. The descriptive text has been kept to a minimum. Yet, with it, you can easily identify the best times of the year to visit your travel destination, or note the months to avoid.

Not everyone is going to agree on what weather is "best." In my definition, the "best" time to travel is when the weather will cause you the least inconvenience—when rainfall is infrequent, temperatures are mild, and humidity is as comfortable as possible. The goal is to pick a time to travel when you won't have to lug around a lot of coats, umbrellas, or foul-weather gear. I believe you should be able to enjoy your trip in the best weather conditions possible so you can get the most out of your travel time and expenses.

About the Tables

The data in the tables was taken from various government publications, both domestic and international. Some of the international data was originally in metric format. It has been converted to English (imperial) units of measurement. The data has been checked very carefully for accuracy. However, no guarantee can be made for the ultimate reliability of the data.

Average High Temperature

The high temperature of the day occurs, on the average, at about 2 to 4 P.M. in most locations. In general, the average temperature you are likely to experience during the afternoon will be within several degrees of the average high.

Average Low Temperature

The low temperature of the day occurs, on the average, around sunrise, or within an hour of it. On rare occasions, a sharp change in airmass will result in cooler temperatures during the day than the night.

Humidity

The descriptive scale for humidity used in this book is based on the average monthly dew point temperature. I decided to present humidity in this way because relative humidity can be confusing (it is relative to the temperature and therefore cannot stand alone as a measure of comfort). Since the dew point temperature is not a familiar concept to most people, the following scale is used throughout this book:

80+	dew point	=	extremely high humidity
70s	dew point	=	very high humidity
60s	dew point	=	high humidity
50s	dew point	=	moderate
40s	dew point	=	low humidity
<40	dew point	=	very low humidity

I think you will find that this scale corresponds well with our subjective experience of humidity. It's based on many years of observation and conversations with people in my capacity as a television meteorologist.

Precipitation Days

This column shows the average number of days during the month with precipitation—either rain or snow. This may be more important than the total precipitation amount, because frequent rainy days can cause more travel problems than a few days with heavy but brief rainfall. In the tropics, it can rain almost every day, but the duration of rainfall is short—often less than an hour. Then the rain stops, and it's back to sunshine again. Rainfall in the middle latitudes can last for many hours, and often all day. Therefore, it's difficult to compare the "raininess" of middle latitude and tropical locations by looking at the number of days with rain. However, it's safe to say that for any given location, the fewer the rainy days, the better your odds for an enjoyable trip.

Precipitation Inches

This column shows the total amount of rainfall plus melted snowfall likely to accumulate for each month. Refer to the discussion above on Precipitation Days.

Snowfall Inches

This column shows the average amount of snow that falls during the month, except for cities where data is not available or where it's too hot to snow. Snowfall totals can vary widely and are quite sensitive to temperature. Much of the information for European stations had to be computed due to gaps in the database. A "T" in the snowfall column indicates trace amounts.

Weather Records

The individual weather records at the bottom of each data page were taken from a variety of sources and are believed to be current. Since weather records are being broken all the time, it's possible that some of these records may be out of date even as they are printed. If you spot one that needs updating, please write in and tell us about the new record so we can add it to the next edition.

Best Time To Travel

In the descriptive text preceding the data tables, I've included the best months to travel. Please refer to page 2 for the definition of "best." I hope you will find this feature a useful aid for efficient trip planning.

Conversion Charts

Fahrenheit-to-Celsius Conversions

°F	0	1	2	3	4	5	6	7	8	9
110	43	44	44	45	46	46	47	47	48	48
100	38	38	39	39	40	41	41	42	42	43
90	32	33	33	34	34	35	36	36	37	37
80	27	27	28	28	29	29	30	31	31	32
70	21	22	22	23	23	24	24	25	26	26
60	16	16	17	17	18	18	19	19	20	21
50	10	11	11	12	12	13	13	14	14	15
40	4	5	6	6	7	7	8	8	9	9
30	-1	-1	0	1	1	2	2	3	3	4
20	-7	-6	-6	-5	-4	-4	-3	-3	-2	-2
10	-12	-12	-11	-11	-10	-9	-9	-8	-8	-7
0	-18	-17	-17	-16	-16	-15	-14	-14	-13	-13
-0	-18	-18	-19	-19	-20	-21	-21	-22	-22	-23
-10	-23	-24	-24	-25	-26	-26	-27	-27	-28	-28
-20	-29	-29	-30	-31	-31	-32	-32	-33	-33	-34
-30	-34	-35	-36	-36	-37	-37	-38	-38	-39	-39
-40	-40	-41	-41	-42	-42	-43	-43	-44	-44	-45
-50	-46	-46	-47	-47	-48	-48	-49	-49	-50	-51

Celsius-to-Fahrenheit Conversions

°C	0	1	2	3	4	5	6	7	8	9
40	104	106	108	109	111	113	115	117	118	120
30	86	88	90	91	93	95	97	99	100	102
20	68	70	72	73	75	77	79	81	82	84
10	50	52	54	55	57	59	61	63	64	66
0	32	34	36	37	39	41	43	45	46	48
-0	32	30	28	27	25	23	21	19	18	16
-10	14	12	10	9	7	5	3	1	-0	-2
-20	-4	-6	-8	-9	-11	-13	-15	-17	-18	-20
-30	-22	-24	-26	-27	-29	-31	-33	-35	-36	-38
-40	-40	-42	-44	-45	-47	-49	-51	-53	-54	-56
-50	-58	-60	-62	-63	-65	-67	-69	-71	-72	-74

Conversions

Length

1 inch (in.)	=	2.54 centimeters or 0.08 feet.
1 meter (m)	=	100 centimeters, 3.28 feet, or 39.37 inches.
1 centimeter (cm)	=	0.39 inch, 0.01 meter, or 10 millimeters.
1 kilometer (km)	=	1000 meters, 3,281 feet, or 0.62 mile.
1 mile (mi)	=	5280 feet, 1609 meters, or 1.61 kilometers.
1 degree latitude	=	111 kilometers or 60 nautical miles.

Volume & Mass

1 liter (l)	=	0.264 gallon (gal)
1 gram (g)	=	0.035 ounce, or 0.002 pound (lb)
1 kilogram (kg)	=	1000 grams or 2.2 pounds

Speed

1 knot	=	1.15 mi/hr or 1.85 km/hr
1 mile per hour	=	0.87 knot or 1.61 km/hr
1 km per hour	=	0.54 knot or 0.62 mi/hr

Pressure

1 millibar (mb)	=	0.75 millimeter of mercury (mm Hg) or 0.02953 inch of mercury (in. Hg)
1 inch of mercury	=	33.865 millibars

U.S. and International Time Zones

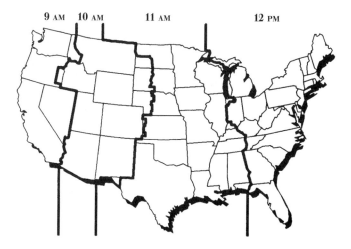

	Time Based On 12 P.M. E.S.T.	Difference in Hours From E.S.T.
NEW YORK	12 Noon	0
Acapulco	11 A.M.	- 1
Athens	7 P.M.	+7
Buenos Aires	2 P.M.	+2
Cairo	7 P.M.	+7
Geneva	6 P.M.	+6
Hong Kong	1 A.M.	+13
Johannesburg	7 P.M.	+7
London	5 P.M.	+5
Madrid	6 P.M.	+6
Manila	1 A.M.	+13
Moscow	8 P.M.	+8
Honolulu	7 A.M.	- 5
Paris	6 P.M.	+6
Rio de Janeiro	2 P.M.	+2
Rome	6 P.M.	+6
Sydney	3 A.M.	+15
Tokyo	2 A.M.	+14
Vancouver	9 A.M.	- 3
Vienna	6 P.M.	+6
Wellington	5 A.M.	+17

Unusual Weather Conditions

Hurricanes

A hurricane is an intense storm of tropical origin with sustained winds of at least 74 miles per hour. Hurricanes that affect the U.S. originate in the Atlantic, the Caribbean Sea, and the eastern North Pacific ocean. These massive storms form over warm, tropical waters, beginning innocently as a group of scattered thunderstorms.

As the storm becomes more "organized" and the winds near the center increase to 75 miles per hour or more, a clear area called the eye forms in the center. Weather in the eye is generally partly cloudy with light winds.

The wall of the eye consists of fierce winds, heavy rain, and often tornadoes. This area is the most intense part of the hurricane. Winds in the eye wall can exceed 155 miles per hour in the bigger storms.

The hurricane season runs from June through November for the Atlantic and Caribbean. However, almost twice as many hurricanes form in the eastern North Pacific. The Atlantic/Caribbean hurricanes generally receive more publicity since they affect the heavily populated U.S. coastline from Texas to Florida, then up to Maine.

Because two or more storms can be present at the same time, they are given names to avoid confusion. In recent years, female and male names have alternated, and the names are different for the Atlantic/Caribbean and the Pacific.

Hurricane Damage Scale

Category	Central Pressure	Winds (MPH)	Storm Surge	Property Damage
1	28.94"	74-95	4-5'	Minimal
2	28.50-28.93"	96-110	6-8'	Moderate
3	27.90-28.49"	111-130	9-12'	Extensive
4	27.17-27.89"	131-155	13-18'	Extensive
5	27.16" or less	156 or more	18.1' or More	Catastrophic

Based on the Saffir/Simpson Damage-Potential Scale

Atlantic Hurricane Names

1996   Arthur, Bertha, Cesar, Dolly, Edouard, Fran, Gustav, Hortense, Isidore, Josephine, Kyle, Lili, Marco, Nana, Omar, Paloma, Rene, Sally, Teddy, Vicky, Wilfred

1997   Ana, Bill, Claudette, Danny, Erika, Fabian, Grace, Henri, Isabell, Juan, Kate, Larry, Mindy, Nicholas, Odette, Peter, Rose, Sam, Teresa, Victor, Wanda

1998   Alex, Bonnie, Charley, Danielle, Earl, Frances, Georges, Hermine, Ivan, Jeanne, Karl, Lisa, Mitch, Nicole, Otto, Paula, Richard, Shary, Tomas, Virginie, Walter

1999   Arlene, Bret, Cindy, Dennis, Emily, Floyd, Gert, Harvey, Irene, Jose, Katrina, Lenny, Maria, Nate, Ophelia, Philippe, Rita, Stan, Tammy, Vince, Wilma

2000   Alberto, Beryl, Chris, Debby, Ernesto, Florence, Gordon, Helene, Isaac, Joyce, Keith, Leslie, Michael, Nadine, Oscar, Patty, Rafael, Sandy, Tony, Valerie, William

Eastern Pacific Hurricane Names

1996   Alma, Boris, Christina, Douglas, Elida, Fausto, Genevieve, Hernan, Iselle, Julio, Kenna, Lowell, Marie, Norbert, Odile, Polo, Rachel, Simon, Trudy, Vance, Wallis, Xavier, Yolanda, Zeke

1997   Andres, Blanca, Carlos, Dolores, Enrique, Felicia, Guillermo, Hilda, Ignacio, Jimena, Kevin, Linda, Marty, Nora, Olaf, Pauline, Rick, Sandra, Terry, Vivian, Waldo, Xina, York, Zelda

1998   Agatha, Blas, Celia, Darby, Estelle, Frank, Georgette, Howard, Isis, Javier, Kay, Lester, Madeline, Newton, Orlene, Paine, Roslyn, Seymour, Tina, Virgil, Winifred, Xavier, Yolanda, Zeke

1999   Adrian, Beatriz, Calvin, Dora, Eugene, Fernanda, Greg, Hilary, Irwin, Jova, Kenneth, Lidia, Max, Norma, Otis, Pilar, Ramon, Selma, Todd, Veronica, Wilfy, Xina, York, Zelda

2000   Aletia, Bud, Carlotta, Daniel, Emilia, Fabio, Gilma, Hector, Ileana, John, Kristy, Lane, Miriam, Norman, Olivia, Paul, Rosa, Sergio, Tara, Vicente, Willa, Xavier, Yolanda, Zeke

Hurricane names are recycled every 6 years.

Thunderstorms & Lightning

Thunderstorms occur over most of the world. In the U.S., they are more severe over mountain areas, the Midwest, the Plains, the South, and the East. They are more likely to occur during the spring and summer months, but can be experienced at any time of year. Although thunderstorms present a spectacular light show, they can be very dangerous. Some result in large hail and high winds that often cause property damage and injuries. Therefore, precautionary steps should be taken if you are caught in a thunderstorm.

Lightning Safety Rules

1. Get inside your home or an automobile that is not a convertible. If possible, avoid using the telephone. Unplug major appliances to prevent possible damage.

2. If you are caught outside, stay in low-lying areas so that you do not project above the immediate environment. Put down golf clubs.

3. Stay away from isolated objects like trees or telephone poles. Do not stand next to metal objects, like wire fences and metal pipes.

4. Get out of, or stay away from, open water.

5. If you're with others, spread out. If your hair is standing straight up, it's a sign that lightning may be about to strike you. Do not lie flat on the ground. Drop to your knees and bend forward putting your hands on your knees.

Estimating How Far the Thunderstorm Is Away From You

If you see lightning, count the number of seconds from the time of the flash until you hear thunder. Divide the number of seconds by five; that's how far away the lightning is in miles.

Tornadoes

Tornadoes are intense low pressure areas with winds that can exceed 200 miles per hour. They begin as funnel clouds, tail-like formations that hang from large thunderstorms. They are classified as tornadoes when the funnel touches the ground. Tornadoes usually form when cold air masses from the north meet warm, moist air masses from the south. They are most likely to form in the late afternoon and early evening, from March to July. However, they have occurred in every month.

Although many parts of the world experience tornadoes, the United States has the highest annual average with more than 700 each year. Every state, including Alaska and Hawaii, has experienced a tornado, but the Central Plains (from Texas to Nebraska) may average as many as 4 tornadoes per day during the tornado season.

There are two types of tornado alerts: a tornado watch and a tornado warning. A tornado watch means that conditions are favorable for tornado formation. A tornado warning means that a tornado has been sighted. If you are in an area that is experiencing a tornado, follow these tips:

1. If you are at home: Stay away from windows and outside walls to avoid flying debris. Try to get to a basement, an inside closet, or a bathroom. Never go above the first floor. Don't panic. Monitor conditions with a radio.

2. If you are in a car: Get out of the car and take cover inside a building or in a low-lying area.

3. If you are in a public building: Stay away from walls and windows, and try to get to the center of the building. Do not use the elevator. Another area of protection is inside stairwells.

Wind Chill

When the wind is blowing, the temperature feels colder than it would feel if the air were still. The combined effects of the wind and temperature create a wind chill temperature that is lower than a thermometer alone would indicate. The faster the wind, the lower the wind chill temperature. This lower "chill" temperature has the same effect on human skin as the equivalent temperature would in calm air. That is, a wind chill of minus 10 degrees has the same effect on a person as an actual temperature of minus 10 degrees with no wind. You might call the wind chill temperature the "no wind" equivalent temperature.

Using the table below, you can determine the wind chill by first finding the actual temperature in the left column, then the wind speed along the top line. The wind chill temperature can be found where the row and column meet in the center. For example, a temperature of 20 degrees with a wind of 10 miles an hour results in a wind chill of 2 degrees.

Wind Speed in Miles Per Hour

		5	10	15	20	25	30	35	40	45	50
	35	33	21	16	12	7	5	3	1	1	0
	30	27	16	11	3	0	-2	-4	-4	-6	-7
	25	21	9	1	-4	-7	-11	-13	-15	-17	-17
	20	16	2	-6	-9	-15	-18	-20	-22	-24	-24
	15	12	-2	-11	-17	-22	-26	-27	-29	-31	-31
	10	7	-9	-18	-24	-29	-33	-35	-36	-38	-38
	5	1	-15	-25	-32	-37	-41	-43	-45	-46	-47
	0	-6	-22	-33	-40	-45	-49	-52	-54	-54	-56
Temperature	**-5**	-11	-27	-40	-46	-52	-56	-60	-62	-63	-63
	-10	-15	-31	-45	-52	-58	-63	-67	-69	-70	-70
	-15	-20	-38	-51	-60	-67	-70	-72	-76	-78	-79
	-20	-26	-45	-60	-68	-75	-78	-83	-87	-87	-88
	-25	-31	-52	-65	-76	-83	-87	-90	-94	-94	-96
	-30	-35	-58	-70	-81	-89	-94	-98	-101	-101	-103
	-35	-41	-64	-78	-88	-96	-101	-105	-107	-108	-110
	-40	-47	-70	-85	-96	-104	-109	-113	-116	-118	-120
	-45	-54	-77	-90	-103	-112	-117	-123	-128	-128	-128

Wind speeds above 50 mph have little additional chilling effect.

Beaufort Wind Scale

Beaufort Number	Explanatory Titles	Land Specifications	Miles Per Hour	Forecast Terms
0	Calm	Smoke rises vertically.	Less Than 1	Light
1	Light Air	Direction of wind shown by smoke drift, but not by wind vanes.	1–3	Light
2	Slight Breeze	Wind felt on face; leaves rustle; ordinary vane moved by wind.	4–7	Light
3	Gentle Breeze	Leaves and small twigs in constant motion; small branches moved.	8–12	Gentle
4	Mod. Breeze	Raises dust and loose paper; small branches are moved.	13–18	Moderate
5	Fresh Breeze	Small trees in leaf begin to sway; crested wavelets form on inland water.	19–24	Fresh

Beaufort Wind Scale — continued

Beaufort Number	Explanatory Titles	Land Specifications	Miles Per Hour	Forecast Terms
6	Strong Breeze	Large branches in motion; whistling; umbrellas used with difficulty.	25–31	Strong
7	High Wind	Whole trees in motion; inconvenience felt in walking against wind.	32–38	Strong
8	Gale	Breaks twigs off trees; generally impedes progress.	39–46	Gale
9	Strong Gale	Slight structural damage occurs (chimney pots and slate removed)	47–54	Gale
10	Whole Gale	Seldom experienced inland; trees uprooted; considerable damage.	55–63	Whole Gale
11	Storm	Very rarely experienced; accompanied by widespread damage.	64–75	Whole Gale
12	Hurricane	Extensive damage.		Hurricane

Winter Travel Guidelines

Weather conditions can change rapidly during the winter, especially in the mountains. To protect yourself from hazardous winter weather, follow these guidelines:

1. Plan your travel route carefully. Be aware of your primary and secondary travel routes.
2. Check the latest weather and road conditions.
3. Fill your gas tank before leaving.
4. If possible, avoid traveling alone.
5. If a storm becomes hazardous, seek refuge.

There are occasions when a storm will catch travelers off guard. If you are caught in a blizzard, follow these instructions:

1. Stay inside your car and avoid exposure to the wind and cold.
2. Keep your window slightly open for ventilation and fresh air.
3. Run your motor and heater sparingly to prevent carbon monoxide poisoning. Avoid draining your car's battery.
4. Do not sleep or stay in one position. Exercise your hands and arms to keep good circulation.
5. Turn on your dome or parking lights to make your car visible, and keep watch.

Earth Science and Astronomy

Earthquakes

The areas of the United States most likely to experience damaging earthquakes are found near the California coast within 50 to 100 miles of the San Andreas Fault, a major crack in the Earth's crust. Strong earthquakes have also occurred in other areas of the country, however.

Earthquakes are measured by two different methods. The first and most famous is the Richter Scale. This scale measures earthquake strength as recorded on a seismograph. Each increase of 1.0 unit on this scale represents an increase in peak strength of 10 times, and an increase of 30 times in total energy released.

In 1811–12, three major earthquakes shook New Madrid, Missouri. Charleston, South Carolina, felt a major quake in 1886, and a massive jolt caused severe damage in Alaska in 1964.

The San Francisco earthquake of 1906 measured 8.3 on the Richter Scale. The 1989 Loma Prieta quake in the San Francisco Bay Area registered 7.1, while the Northridge (Los Angeles) quake of 1994 measured 6.7. A jolt of at least 5.5 is needed to produce significant damage near the "epicenter" of a quake.

Earthquake Safety Tips

1. If you're inside a building, stand under a doorway, or get under a table, desk, or bed. Stay away from tall furniture and windows, and do not rush outside.

2. If you're in a crowded building, don't go to the exits, because many other people will be doing so. If possible, get under a sturdy object, then choose an exit when it's safe.

3. If you're outside, stay away from high buildings, walls, and power lines. Try to get to an open area.

4. If you're in a car, pull over to the side of the road and stay inside.

5. Don't light a match to check for gas leaks after the earthquake.

Richter Magnitudes

Less than 2.5	Generally not felt, but recorded. Estimated 900,000 per year.
2.5 to 5.4	Often felt, but only minor damage detected. Estimated 30,000 per year.
5.5 to 6.0	Slight damage to structures. Estimated 500 per year.
6.1 to 6.9	Can be destructive in populous regions. Estimated 100 per year.
7.0 to 7.9	Major earthquakes. Inflict serious damage. Estimated 20 per year.
8.0 or greater	Great earthquakes. Produce total destruction to communities near epicenter. One every 5 to 10 years.

Eclipses

Lunar Eclipses

Total lunar eclipses can be seen over most of the world on the following dates:

Sept. 27, 1996	May 16, 2003
Sept. 16, 1997	Nov. 9, 2003
Jan. 21, 2000	May 4, 2004
July 16, 2000	Oct. 28, 2004
Jan. 9, 2001	

Solar Eclipses

- *March 9, 1997*—Total over Siberia, Mongolia. Partial over most of East Asia, North Pacific, and Alaska.

- *February 26, 1998*—Total over Panama, northern South America, and the Caribbean. Partial over much of United States, Mexico, and Central and South America.

- *August 11, 1999*—Total over Central Europe from southwest England to northern France, through Austria, then to India. Partial over all of the North Atlantic and all of Europe and most of North Africa across to India.

- *June 21, 2001*—Total over south central Africa to Madagascar. Partial over eastern South America and most of Africa.

- *December 4, 2002*—Total over southern Africa and coast of Western Australia. Partial over most of central and southern Africa and most of Western Australia.

- *November 23, 2003*—Briefly total over Antarctica. Partial over Antarctica to Australia.

Meteors

A meteor is a little sand grain or pebble that strikes our atmosphere and burns up. The light during entry is often called a shooting star. Meteors rarely strike the earth. If they do, they are called meteorites.

Most meteors originate as comets. The nucleus of a comet gradually disintegrates each time it nears the sun. Particles are shed by this nucleus and continue traveling in the same orbit. Eventually, some of these particles spread out along the comet's path. If the path of the Earth crosses this stream of particles, we experience a meteor shower.

All meteors of a shower arrive from the same direction at the same speed. Therefore, they seem to come from the same part of the sky (called its radiant). A shower is named for the constellation from which it radiates. More meteors can be seen in the hours just before dawn.

Over thousands of years, a meteor stream will gradually disperse due to the gravitational pull of the planets. The shower will then become diffuse—the number of meteors declines, and the shower spreads out over weeks instead of hours or days. A meteor that doesn't belong to a shower is called sporadic.

While in space, particles are called meteoroids. When one strikes the atmosphere with a brief streak of light, it is called a meteor. A very bright meteor is called a fireball, and an exploding meteor is called a bolide. Some of the brightest ones leave glowing trains of luminous smoke. A meteor's brightness depends on its size, speed, composition, and the angle at which it hits the atmosphere. A fireball may start out as a particle that weighs only one ounce.

Major Meteor Showers

Shower	Date(s)	Z.H.R.	No. Days
Quadrantids	Jan. 3–4	50–120	0.4
Lyrids	Apr. 22	15–25	1
Eta Aquarids	May 4	60	6
S. Delta Aquarids	Jul. 29	30	8
N. Delta Aquarids	Aug. 12	20	8?
Perseids	Aug. 12	60–120	3
Orionids	Oct. 21	30	1.6
Southern Taurids	Nov. 3	15	30?
Northern Taurids	Nov. 13	15	30?
Leonids	Nov. 17	15	Var.
Geminids	Dec. 13–14	90	1.5
Ursids	Dec. 22	15	2

Z.H.R. = Zenith Hourly Rate (Number that would be seen per hour by an experienced watcher in a dark sky)

Part I

United States
Canada
Mexico

CHAPTER 1

United States

ALASKA

A number of definite statements can be made about Alaska. It is extremely beautiful. There's much to see and do. It can get brutally cold. However, it's not always cold. In fact, summertime in Alaska can be warm, and occasionally hot.

First, the humidity—there isn't much of it, so it's not a factor to be concerned about. Temperatures *are* a critical factor in planning your trip to Alaska. The warmest months occur, of course, in the summer. June, July, and August are really the only warm months. In the interior, temperatures can climb to 90 degrees in July. Along the coast, summer temperatures remain cool because of the moderating influence of water in the Gulf of Alaska. The best time to visit Alaska is June. Temperatures are nearly at their peak, the days are very long—in some areas 24 hours long—and rainfall is moderate.

Rainfall increases later in the summer, peaking in August in Fairbanks and September in Anchorage. By September the days are chilly and the nights cold. By October it feels like winter everywhere in Alaska. And after that, well, it's just cold, but beautiful, as only an Alaskan winter can be.

ALASKA

A N C H O R A G E — 114 ft.

	JAN	FEB	MAR	APR	MAY	JUN	JUL	AUG	SEP	OCT	NOV	DEC	ANN.
Av. High °F	20	27	33	44	55	63	66	64	56	42	28	21	43
Av. Low °F	4	9	15	27	37	46	50	48	40	28	14	5	27
Humidity	V.Lo	V.Lo	V.Lo	V.Lo	V.Lo	Lo	Lo	Lo	Lo	V.Lo	V.Lo	V.Lo	V.Lo
Precip. Days	6	9	8	7	7	8	11	12	13	11	10	11	113
Precip. In.	.8	.8	.6	.6	.6	1.1	2.1	2.3	2.4	1.4	1.0	1.1	14.8
Snowfall In.	11	12	9	6	1	0	0	0	<1	6	10	15	70

F A I R B A N K S — 440 ft.

	JAN	FEB	MAR	APR	MAY	JUN	JUL	AUG	SEP	OCT	NOV	DEC	ANN.
Av. High °F	-2	9	23	40	59	71	72	66	54	34	12	-2	36
Av. Low °F	-22	-14	-4	17	36	47	50	45	34	17	-6	-19	15
Humidity	V.Lo	V.Lo	V.Lo	V.Lo	V.Lo	Lo	Lo	Lo	V.Lo	V.Lo	V.Lo	V.Lo	V.Lo
Precip. Days	7	7	7	5	6	10	12	12	9	10	9	8	102
Precip. In.	.6	.5	.5	.3	.7	1.4	1.9	2.2	1.1	.7	.7	.6	11.2
Snowfall In.	11	9	8	4	1	0	0	0	1	10	13	12	69

HIGHEST U.S. & NORTH AMERICAN
SEA LEVEL PRESSURE: 31.74"
Northway, Alaska — January 31, 1989

THE EAST

Eastern weather is known for its variety. Unlike the West, where the climate can change radically from city to city, the East has definite, memorable, genuine seasons. Summers are warm and humid, falls are colorful, winters are cold with snow, and springs are changeable with everything in bloom—it's all right out of the textbooks.

Since weather systems generally move from west to east, almost all storms that start somewhere else in the country will eventually end up somewhere in the East. This includes cold Canadian winter air masses and milder Pacific storms that move all the way across the continent in a matter of days. The East often ends up with rain from "lows" that form in the Gulf of Mexico. Even hurricanes that start far out in the Atlantic can strike the East Coast somewhere between Cape Hatteras and New England.

East Coast weather is strongly influenced by the Gulf Stream, that warm current of tropical, warm water that flows from South Florida, up the Atlantic seaboard, then out into the North Atlantic. Because of the stream's warmth, the East has milder temperatures in the winter than midwestern states at the same latitude. This same warm water current can add quite a bit of humidity to the air masses that affect the eastern states, and the result can be heavy rainfall in any month. In fact, there really is no dominant rainy season in the East. However, a bit more rain does fall in the summer than the winter because of the added moisture content of the summertime air.

The long mountain ranges that separate the Atlantic coastal plain from the Midwest—the Green Mountains and Adirondacks in the North, and the Appalachians farther south—also help to isolate the East to some extent from the extremes of Midwestern air masses and storms. In particular, the mountains interfere with the crosscurrents of air needed to produce tornadoes, and hence act as a barrier that keeps the number of tornadoes that strike from D.C. to New England to a minimum.

Eastern summer weather can be very warm and humid, especially during July and August. All factors considered, late May and early June and the month of September are just about ideal times to take a trip to the East. If it's sheer beauty you are looking for, the peak of fall can be enjoyed in October.

If you love to ski, head for New England in the winter. And if you love to see nature at its finest, you might enjoy a visit during spring. So what's wrong with summer? Head for New England and have a great time.

CONNECTICUT

H A R T F O R D — 169 ft.

	JAN	FEB	MAR	APR	MAY	JUN	JUL	AUG	SEP	OCT	NOV	DEC	ANN.
Av. High °F	33	36	45	59	70	80	84	82	75	64	51	37	60
Av. Low °F	16	18	27	37	46	56	61	59	51	41	32	20	39
Humidity	V.Lo	V.Lo	V.Lo	V.Lo	Lo	Med	Hi	Hi	Med	Lo	V.Lo	V.Lo	Lo
Precip. Days	11	11	11	11	12	11	10	10	10	8	11	13	129
Precip. In.	3.3	3.2	3.9	3.7	3.5	3.5	3.4	4.0	3.5	3.0	4.3	4.1	43.4
Snowfall In.	11	13	12	2	0	0	0	0	0	0	2	13	53

GREATEST U.S. PRECIPITATION IN ONE MINUTE: 1.2"
Unionville, Maryland — July 4, 1956

DISTRICT OF COLUMBIA

WASHINGTON, D. C. — 72 ft.

	JAN	FEB	MAR	APR	MAY	JUN	JUL	AUG	SEP	OCT	NOV	DEC	ANN.
Av. High °F	41	45	53	65	75	83	86	85	79	68	56	43	65
Av. Low °F	23	24	31	41	51	59	64	62	55	44	34	25	43
Humidity	V.Lo	V.Lo	V.Lo	Lo	Med	Hi	Hi	Hi	Med	Lo	V.Lo	V.Lo	Lo
Precip. Days	10	9	10	10	12	9	10	9	8	7	8	10	112
Precip. In.	2.8	2.6	3.5	3.0	3.7	3.6	4.1	4.2	3.3	2.7	3.1	3.5	40.1
Snowfall In.	5	7	3	<1	0	0	0	0	0	0	2	6	23

MAINE

PORTLAND — 43 ft.

	JAN	FEB	MAR	APR	MAY	JUN	JUL	AUG	SEP	OCT	NOV	DEC	ANN.
Av. High °F	31	33	41	53	64	73	79	78	70	60	48	35	55
Av. Low °F	12	13	23	33	42	51	57	55	47	38	30	16	35
Humidity	V.Lo	V.Lo	V.Lo	V.Lo	Lo	Med	Med	Med	Lo	V.Lo	V.Lo	V.Lo	V.Lo
Precip. Days	11	10	11	12	13	11	9	9	8	9	12	12	127
Precip. In.	3.4	3.5	3.6	3.5	3.3	3.1	2.6	2.6	3.1	3.3	4.9	4.1	40.8
Snowfall In.	18	20	14	3	<1	0	0	0	0	<1	3	16	74

MARYLAND

BALTIMORE — 14 ft.

	JAN	FEB	MAR	APR	MAY	JUN	JUL	AUG	SEP	OCT	NOV	DEC	ANN.
Av. High °F	42	44	53	65	75	83	87	85	79	68	56	44	65
Av. Low °F	25	26	33	42	53	62	67	65	58	46	36	27	45
Humidity	V.Lo	V.Lo	V.Lo	Lo	Med	Hi	Hi	Hi	Med	Lo	V.Lo	V.Lo	Lo
Precip. Days	10	9	11	11	11	9	9	10	8	7	9	9	113
Precip. In.	2.9	2.8	3.7	3.1	3.6	3.8	4.1	4.2	3.1	2.8	3.1	3.3	40.5
Snowfall In.	5	6	5	<1	0	0	0	0	0	0	1	5	22

MASSACHUSETTS

BOSTON — 124 ft.

	JAN	FEB	MAR	APR	MAY	JUN	JUL	AUG	SEP	OCT	NOV	DEC	ANN.
Av. High °F	36	38	45	56	67	77	81	79	72	63	52	39	59
Av. Low °F	23	23	32	41	50	59	65	63	57	48	39	27	44
Humidity	V.Lo	V.Lo	V.Lo	V.Lo	Lo	Med	Hi	Hi	Lo	Med	V.Lo	V.Lo	V.Lo
Precip. Days	12	11	12	11	12	11	9	10	9	9	11	12	129
Precip. In.	3.7	3.5	4.0	3.5	3.5	3.2	2.7	3.5	3.2	3.0	4.5	4.2	42.5
Snowfall In.	12	12	8	1	0	0	0	0	0	0	1	8	42

NEW HAMPSHIRE

CONCORD — 342 ft.

	JAN	FEB	MAR	APR	MAY	JUN	JUL	AUG	SEP	OCT	NOV	DEC	ANN.
Av. High °F	31	34	42	57	69	78	83	80	72	62	48	35	58
Av. Low °F	10	11	22	32	42	52	57	54	47	36	28	15	34
Humidity	V.Lo	V.Lo	V.Lo	V.Lo	Lo	Med	Med	Med	Med	V.Lo	V.Lo	V.Lo	V.Lo
Precip. Days	11	10	11	11	12	11	10	10	9	8	11	11	125
Precip. In.	2.7	2.4	2.8	2.9	3.0	3.3	3.1	2.9	3.1	2.7	4.0	3.3	36.2
Snowfall In.	17	16	11	2	<1	0	0	0	0	<1	4	14	64

NEW JERSEY

ATLANTIC CITY — 64 ft.

	JAN	FEB	MAR	APR	MAY	JUN	JUL	AUG	SEP	OCT	NOV	DEC	ANN.
Av. High °F	41	43	51	62	72	81	85	83	77	68	56	44	64
Av. Low °F	24	25	32	41	51	60	65	64	57	46	36	26	44
Humidity	V.Lo	V.Lo	V.Lo	Lo	Med	Hi	Hi	Hi	Med	Lo	V.Lo	V.Lo	Lo
Precip. Days	11	10	11	11	10	9	9	9	8	7	9	9	113
Precip. In.	3.6	3.4	4.3	3.4	3.5	3.4	4.3	4.9	3.0	3.5	4.2	4.0	45.5
Snowfall In.	5	5	3	<1	0	0	0	0	0	0	<1	2	16

TRENTON — 56 ft.

	JAN	FEB	MAR	APR	MAY	JUN	JUL	AUG	SEP	OCT	NOV	DEC	ANN.
Av. High °F	39	41	49	62	72	81	85	83	76	66	54	42	62
Av. Low °F	25	26	33	43	52	62	67	65	58	48	39	28	46
Humidity	V.Lo	V.Lo	V.Lo	V.Lo	Med	Med	Hi	Hi	Med	Lo	V.Lo	V.Lo	Lo
Precip. Days	11	10	12	11	12	10	10	10	8	8	10	11	123
Precip. In.	2.8	2.7	3.8	3.1	3.4	3.2	4.7	4.2	3.2	2.5	3.3	3.3	40.2
Snowfall In.	6	7	4	1	0	0	0	0	0	<1	<1	5	23

NEW YORK

ALBANY — 275 ft.

	JAN	FEB	MAR	APR	MAY	JUN	JUL	AUG	SEP	OCT	NOV	DEC	ANN.
Av. High °F	30	33	43	58	70	79	84	81	74	63	48	34	58
Av. Low °F	13	14	24	36	46	56	60	58	50	40	31	18	37
Humidity	V.Lo	V.Lo	V.Lo	V.Lo	Lo	Med	Hi	Med	Med	Lo	V.Lo	V.Lo	V.Lo
Precip. Days	13	11	12	12	13	11	11	10	9	9	12	13	136
Precip. In.	2.2	2.1	2.6	2.7	3.3	3.0	3.1	2.9	3.1	2.6	2.8	2.9	33.3
Snowfall In.	15	15	12	3	0	0	0	0	0	<1	4	16	65

B U F F A L O — 705 ft.

	JAN	FEB	MAR	APR	MAY	JUN	JUL	AUG	SEP	OCT	NOV	DEC	ANN.
Av. High °F	30	31	39	53	64	75	80	78	71	60	46	34	55
Av. Low °F	18	18	25	36	46	56	61	59	52	43	34	22	39
Humidity	V.Lo	V.Lo	V.Lo	V.Lo	Lo	Med	Med	Med	Med	Lo	V.Lo	V.Lo	V.Lo
Precip. Days	20	17	16	14	13	10	10	10	10	11	16	20	167
Precip. In.	2.9	2.5	2.9	3.2	3.0	2.2	2.9	3.5	3.3	3.0	3.7	3.0	36.1
Snowfall In.	22	18	12	3	<1	0	0	0	0	<1	13	22	90

N E W   Y O R K   C I T Y — 132 ft.

	JAN	FEB	MAR	APR	MAY	JUN	JUL	AUG	SEP	OCT	NOV	DEC	ANN.
Av. High °F	39	40	48	61	71	81	85	83	77	67	54	41	62
Av. Low °F	26	27	34	44	53	63	68	66	60	51	41	30	47
Humidity	V.Lo	V.Lo	V.Lo	V.Lo	Lo	Med	Hi	Hi	Med	Lo	V.Lo	V.Lo	Lo
Precip. Days	11	10	12	11	11	10	11	10	8	8	9	10	121
Precip. In.	2.7	2.9	3.7	3.3	3.5	3.0	3.7	4.0	3.3	2.8	3.8	3.5	40.2
Snowfall In.	7	9	5	1	0	0	0	0	0	0	1	6	29

PENNSYLVANIA

P H I L A D E L P H I A — 26 ft.

	JAN	FEB	MAR	APR	MAY	JUN	JUL	AUG	SEP	OCT	NOV	DEC	ANN.
Av. High °F	40	42	51	64	74	83	87	85	78	68	56	43	64
Av. Low °F	24	26	33	42	52	62	67	65	58	47	37	27	45
Humidity	V.Lo	V.Lo	V.Lo	V.Lo	Lo	Med	Hi	Hi	Med	Lo	V.Lo	V.Lo	Lo
Precip. Days	11	9	11	11	11	10	9	9	8	7	9	10	115
Precip. In.	2.8	2.6	3.7	3.3	3.4	3.7	4.1	4.1	3.0	2.5	3.4	3.3	39.9
Snowfall In.	5	6	4	<1	0	0	0	0	0	0	1	4	20

P I T T S B U R G H — 1,137 ft.

	JAN	FEB	MAR	APR	MAY	JUN	JUL	AUG	SEP	OCT	NOV	DEC	ANN.
Av. High °F	37	40	49	63	72	81	84	83	77	66	52	40	62
Av. Low °F	24	24	32	43	52	62	65	63	56	45	37	27	44
Humidity	V.Lo	V.Lo	V.Lo	V.Lo	Lo	Med	Hi	Hi	Med	Lo	V.Lo	V.Lo	Lo
Precip. Days	15	14	15	14	13	12	11	9	9	10	12	14	148
Precip. In.	2.6	2.3	3.6	3.4	3.6	3.7	3.8	3.2	2.5	2.5	2.5	2.5	36.2
Snowfall In.	7	7	6	1	0	0	0	0	0	<1	3	6	30

GREATEST GLOBAL RECORDED WIND SPEED: 231 MPH
Mount Washington, New Hampshire — April 12, 1934

RHODE ISLAND

P R O V I D E N C E — 51 ft.

	JAN	FEB	MAR	APR	MAY	JUN	JUL	AUG	SEP	OCT	NOV	DEC	ANN.
Av. High °F	36	38	45	57	67	76	81	80	73	64	52	40	59
Av. Low °F	21	21	29	38	47	57	63	61	54	43	35	23	41
Humidity	V.Lo	V.Lo	V.Lo	V.Lo	Lo	Med	Hi	Hi	Med	Lo	V.Lo	V.Lo	Lo
Precip. Days	11	11	12	11	11	11	9	10	9	8	11	12	126
Precip. In.	3.5	3.5	4.0	3.7	3.5	2.6	2.9	3.9	3.3	3.3	4.5	4.1	42.8
Snowfall In.	9	10	9	1	0	0	0	0	0	<1	<1	8	38

VERMONT

B U R L I N G T O N — 332 ft.

	JAN	FEB	MAR	APR	MAY	JUN	JUL	AUG	SEP	OCT	NOV	DEC	ANN.
Av. High °F	26	28	38	53	66	77	81	78	70	59	44	30	54
Av. Low °F	8	9	20	33	44	54	59	56	49	39	30	15	35
Humidity	V.Lo	V.Lo	V.Lo	V.Lo	Lo	Med	Med	Med	Med	Lo	V.Lo	V.Lo	V.Lo
Precip. Days	14	12	13	12	14	12	12	12	12	11	14	15	153
Precip. In.	1.7	1.7	1.9	2.6	3.0	3.5	3.5	3.7	3.1	2.7	2.9	2.2	32.5
Snowfall In.	18	18	12	4	0	0	0	0	0	<1	7	20	79

GREATEST U.S. SNOWFALL IN 24 HOURS: 76.0"
Silverlake, Colorado — April 14 to 15, 1921

HAWAII

Hawaii is famous for many things, and its weather is certainly at the top of the list. However, it does rain often, which keeps the flowers growing in abundance, but also means it can rain on your trip. It's important to understand that there are wet and dry seasons in the islands and that rainfall varies considerably from one part of each island to another.

Temperatures in Hawaii are generally warm, and it *is* somewhat humid. Winters average about eight degrees cooler than summers, but even in the winter, afternoon temperatures near 80 degrees are just about "perfect."

Rainfall increases during the winter months. The likelihood of cloudy, showery, humid days, with the trade winds absent, increases in October. By November it rains more often; this type of weather can continue until April. Long stretches of mild, sunny, breezy days can be enjoyed all winter long, however. The pattern of winter rainfall is partly reversed on the Big Island of Hawaii, where the moist trade winds of summer are forced upward as they encounter the massive volcanic peaks of Mauna Kea and Mauna Loa. There, it rains more in the summer, but this is an exception in the island chain.

You should also be aware of the fact that areas facing toward the east and northeast ("windward" or toward the prevailing trade winds) are wetter than the "leeward" (west- and southwest-facing) shores. Also, the closer to the mountains you get, the wetter it will be on any given day. It's also cooler by several degrees as you drive or hike up into the lush, tropical Hawaiian mountains. There really isn't a "bad" month weatherwise in Hawaii, but for the best combination of moderate temperature and humidity, infrequent rainfall, and plenty of sunshine, May is probably your best bet. Aloha.

HAWAII (The Big Island)

H I L O — 36 ft.

	JAN	FEB	MAR	APR	MAY	JUN	JUL	AUG	SEP	OCT	NOV	DEC	ANN
Av. High °F	79	79	79	79	81	82	83	83	84	83	81	79	81
Av. Low °F	63	63	64	65	66	67	68	69	68	68	66	64	66
Humidity	Hi	Hi	Hi	Hi	Hi	Hi	Hi	Hi	Hi	Hi	Hi	Hi	Hi
Precip. Days	17	17	23	25	26	24	27	26	23	24	23	21	276
Precip. In.	9.8	12.0	13.3	14.1	9.8	6.1	9.6	10.0	7.8	10.0	15.1	12.8	130.1

K O N A — 18 ft.

	JAN	FEB	MAR	APR	MAY	JUN	JUL	AUG	SEP	OCT	NOV	DEC	ANN.
Av. High °F	81	81	81	82	82	83	84	85	85	85	83	82	83
Av. Low °F	65	65	65	66	68	69	69	70	70	69	68	65	67
Humidity	Hi	Hi	Hi	Hi	Hi	Hi	Hi	Hi	Hi	Hi	Hi	Hi	Hi
Precip. Days	10	7	8	7	8	7	8	8	7	6	7	7	90
Precip. In.	3.1	1.7	2.1	1.6	2.3	2.2	2.5	2.4	1.7	1.7	1.8	1.7	24.8

KAUAI

L I H U E — 103 ft.

	JAN	FEB	MAR	APR	MAY	JUN	JUL	AUG	SEP	OCT	NOV	DEC	ANN.
Av. High °F	78	78	78	79	81	83	84	85	85	83	81	78	81
Av. Low °F	65	65	66	68	70	72	73	74	73	72	70	67	70
Humidity	Hi	Hi	Hi	Hi	Hi	Hi	Hi	Hi	Hi	Hi	Hi	Hi	Hi
Precip. Days	15	14	17	17	16	16	19	18	16	18	18	17	201
Precip. In.	5.9	3.6	4.3	3.1	2.7	1.5	2.2	2.0	2.2	4.4	5.5	5.3	42.8

MAUI

K A H U L U I — 48 ft.

	JAN	FEB	MAR	APR	MAY	JUN	JUL	AUG	SEP	OCT	NOV	DEC	ANN.
Av. High °F	80	80	81	82	84	86	87	88	88	86	84	81	84
Av. Low °F	64	63	65	66	67	69	71	71	70	69	68	65	67
Humidity	Hi	Hi	Hi	Hi	Hi	Hi	Hi	Hi	Hi	Hi	Hi	Hi	Hi
Precip. Days	11	10	11	11	6	5	6	6	5	7	10	11	99
Precip. In.	4.2	2.9	2.6	1.8	.8	.3	.4	.5	.3	1.2	2.5	3.1	20.6

L A H A I N A — 12 ft.

	JAN	FEB	MAR	APR	MAY	JUN	JUL	AUG	SEP	OCT	NOV	DEC	ANN.
Av. High °F	81	81	82	83	86	88	88	89	89	88	85	82	85
Av. Low °F	62	62	63	64	66	68	69	69	69	68	66	64	66
Humidity	Hi	Hi	Hi	Hi	Hi	Hi	Hi	Hi	Hi	Hi	Hi	Hi	Hi
Precip. Days	10	12	8	9	5	5	7	6	5	7	9	10	93
Precip. In.	2.8	2.3	2.3	1.3	.5	.1	.2	.6	.3	1.2	1.6	2.7	15.9

OAHU

H O N O L U L U — 38 ft.

	JAN	FEB	MAR	APR	MAY	JUN	JUL	AUG	SEP	OCT	NOV	DEC	ANN.
Av. High °F	79	79	80	81	84	86	87	87	87	86	83	80	83
Av. Low °F	65	65	66	68	70	72	73	74	73	72	70	67	70
Humidity	Hi	Hi	Hi	Hi	Hi	Hi	Hi	Hi	Hi	Hi	Hi	Hi	Hi
Precip. Days	10	10	9	9	7	6	8	7	7	9	10	10	102
Precip. In.	4.4	2.5	3.2	1.3	1.0	.3	.6	.7	.7	1.5	3.0	3.7	22.9

GREATEST U.S. PRECIPITATION IN 1 CALENDAR YEAR: 704.83"
Puu Kukui, Maui, Hawaii — 1982

THE MIDWEST AND PLAINS

If you like wild weather, you'll like it in the Midwest. Wild means hot one day, cold the next. It means very dry one month and very wet the next, and in no particular order. It means tornadoes, hurricanes (and what they leave behind), bitter cold, sweltering heat, and, of course, lots of thunderstorms. Why does all this occur in the Midwest—at least more than it occurs in other parts of the country?

First of all, the Midwest is in the middle—that is, away from the oceans. Any body of water modifies and "smoothes out" the climate of nearby land masses. An ocean, for example, will act to keep adjacent land cooler in the summer and warmer in the winter than it would be otherwise. And since the Midwest is by definition away from any ocean, its climate tends to be rather unmodified—not "smoothed out." This area gets the full brunt of cold Canadian air masses in the winter, and warm, humid air masses off the Gulf of Mexico in the summer. Often, these two very different air masses clash, and the result is a variety of strong and often disagreeable weather, primarily major storms.

The newest term for large storm systems that appear to cover several Midwest states all at the same time is "Mesoscale Convective Complex"—in other words, masses of large thunderstorms all joined together to bring their destructive fury down on large numbers of people and places all at the same time.

And all of this is thanks to the clash of the wildly different air masses just described.

Some Midwestern cities are near large bodies of water (the Great Lakes), and their climates are modified by these expanses of fresh water. Milwaukee, Chicago, and Detroit are the biggest of these cities, but the lakes are surrounded by smaller cities and towns, all enjoying this modified climate.

As you go farther north in the Midwest and get closer to Canada, the climate becomes cooler and less humid. The coldest temperatures in the country often can be found in North Dakota and Minnesota in the winter.

A trip southward, toward Texas and Louisiana, brings you closer to the warm waters of the Gulf, and the climate becomes milder, at least in terms of temperature. Humidity increases, and so does rainfall.

Tornado season in the Midwest starts before winter is over in the states near the Gulf, and progresses slowly toward the north, reaching the Great Lakes states by early summer.

The best overall combination of moderate temperature and humidity, infrequent rainfall and thunderstorms, and lack of cold "waves" can be found in late summer or early fall. September is probably the ideal month to visit the Midwest.

ILLINOIS

CHICAGO — 823 ft.

	JAN	FEB	MAR	APR	MAY	JUN	JUL	AUG	SEP	OCT	NOV	DEC	ANN.
Av. High °F	31	34	45	59	70	79	83	82	75	66	48	35	59
Av. Low °F	15	18	27	38	47	57	61	60	52	42	30	19	39
Humidity	V.Lo	V.Lo	V.Lo	V.Lo	Lo	Med	Hi	Hi	Med	Lo	V.Lo	V.Lo	V.Lo
Precip. Days	11	10	13	12	11	11	10	8	10	9	10	11	126
Precip. In.	1.7	1.3	2.5	3.4	3.4	4.2	3.5	2.7	3.0	2.3	2.1	1.6	31.7
Snowfall In.	10	8	8	2	<1	0	0	0	0	<1	2	8	38

SPRINGFIELD — 588 ft.

	JAN	FEB	MAR	APR	MAY	JUN	JUL	AUG	SEP	OCT	NOV	DEC	ANN.
Av. High °F	35	39	49	64	74	83	87	85	79	68	51	38	63
Av. Low °F	19	22	30	43	53	63	66	64	56	45	33	23	43
Humidity	V.Lo	V.Lo	V.Lo	Lo	Lo	Hi	Hi	Hi	Med	Lo	V.Lo	V.Lo	Lo
Precip. Days	9	9	12	12	11	10	9	8	9	7	9	10	115
Precip. In.	1.8	1.8	2.7	4.1	3.5	4.2	3.8	2.7	3.3	3.1	2.1	1.9	35.0
Snowfall In.	5	6	4	1	0	0	0	0	0	0	2	5	22

INDIANA

INDIANAPOLIS — 718 ft.

	JAN	FEB	MAR	APR	MAY	JUN	JUL	AUG	SEP	OCT	NOV	DEC	ANN.
Av. High °F	36	39	49	63	73	82	85	84	78	67	51	39	62
Av. Low °F	20	22	30	42	52	61	65	62	55	44	33	23	42
Humidity	V.Lo	V.Lo	V.Lo	Lo	Med	Hi	Hi	Hi	Med	Lo	V.Lo	V.Lo	Lo
Precip. Days	11	10	13	12	12	10	9	8	8	8	10	12	123
Precip. In.	2.8	2.4	3.7	3.9	4.1	4.2	3.7	2.8	2.9	2.5	3.1	2.7	38.8
Snowfall In.	5	5	4	<1	0	0	0	0	0	0	2	5	21

IOWA

DES MOINES — 938 ft.

	JAN	FEB	MAR	APR	MAY	JUN	JUL	AUG	SEP	OCT	NOV	DEC	ANN.
Av. High °F	28	33	43	60	71	80	85	83	75	65	46	33	58
Av. Low °F	11	16	25	39	51	61	65	63	54	44	29	17	40
Humidity	V.Lo	V.Lo	V.Lo	V.Lo	Lo	Hi	Hi	Hi	Med	Lo	V.Lo	V.Lo	V.Lo
Precip. Days	7	7	10	10	11	11	9	9	9	7	6	7	103
Precip. In.	1.1	1.1	2.3	3.0	4.2	4.9	3.3	3.3	3.1	2.1	1.4	1.1	30.9
Snowfall In.	8	7	7	2	0	0	0	0	0	<1	3	6	33

KANSAS

WICHITA — 1,321 ft.

	JAN	FEB	MAR	APR	MAY	JUN	JUL	AUG	SEP	OCT	NOV	DEC	ANN.
Av. High °F	41	47	55	68	77	87	92	91	82	71	56	44	68
Av. Low °F	21	25	32	45	55	65	70	68	59	48	34	25	46
Humidity	V.Lo	V.Lo	V.Lo	Lo	Med	Hi	Hi	Hi	Med	Lo	V.Lo	V.Lo	Lo
Precip. Days	5	5	7	8	10	9	8	7	8	6	5	6	84
Precip. In.	.8	1.0	1.8	2.9	3.6	4.5	4.4	3.1	3.7	2.5	1.2	1.1	30.6
Snowfall In.	4	4	3	<1	0	0	0	0	0	<1	1	3	16

MICHIGAN

DETROIT — 619 ft.

	JAN	FEB	MAR	APR	MAY	JUN	JUL	AUG	SEP	OCT	NOV	DEC	ANN.
Av. High °F	32	34	43	58	69	79	83	82	74	63	48	35	58
Av. Low °F	19	20	28	39	48	59	63	62	55	45	34	24	41
Humidity	V.Lo	V.Lo	V.Lo	V.Lo	Lo	Med	Hi	Med	Med	Lo	V.Lo	V.Lo	V.Lo
Precip. Days	13	12	13	12	12	11	9	9	9	9	11	13	133
Precip. In.	1.9	1.8	2.3	3.1	3.4	3.1	3.0	3.0	2.3	2.5	2.3	2.2	30.9
Snowfall In.	8	8	5	1	0	0	0	0	0	0	3	7	32

GRAND RAPIDS — 784 ft.

	JAN	FEB	MAR	APR	MAY	JUN	JUL	AUG	SEP	OCT	NOV	DEC	ANN.
Av. High °F	30	33	42	57	69	79	83	82	74	63	46	34	58
Av. Low °F	16	16	24	36	45	56	60	58	51	41	31	21	38
Humidity	V.Lo	V.Lo	V.Lo	V.Lo	Lo	Med	Med	Med	Med	Lo	V.Lo	V.Lo	V.Lo
Precip. Days	16	12	13	12	11	11	9	9	10	10	14	17	144
Precip. In.	1.9	1.5	2.5	3.4	3.2	3.4	3.1	2.5	3.3	2.6	2.8	2.2	32.4
Snowfall In.	21	12	13	4	0	0	0	0	0	1	9	17	77

MINNESOTA

MINNEAPOLIS/ST. PAUL — 830 ft.

	JAN	FEB	MAR	APR	MAY	JUN	JUL	AUG	SEP	OCT	NOV	DEC	ANN.
Av. High °F	21	26	37	56	68	77	82	81	71	61	41	27	54
Av. Low °F	3	7	20	35	46	57	61	60	49	39	24	11	34
Humidity	V.Lo	V.Lo	V.Lo	V.Lo	Lo	Med	Hi	Med	Med	Lo	V.Lo	V.Lo	V.Lo
Precip. Days	9	7	10	10	12	12	10	9	9	8	8	9	113
Precip. In.	.7	.8	1.7	2.0	3.4	3.9	3.7	3.1	2.7	1.8	1.2	.9	25.9
Snowfall In.	9	8	11	3	<1	0	0	0	<1	<1	6	9	46

MISSOURI

KANSAS CITY — 742 ft.

	JAN	FEB	MAR	APR	MAY	JUN	JUL	AUG	SEP	OCT	NOV	DEC	ANN.
Av. High °F	36	42	51	65	74	83	88	87	79	69	53	40	64
Av. Low °F	19	24	32	45	56	65	70	68	59	48	35	24	45
Humidity	V.Lo	V.Lo	V.Lo	Lo	Med	Hi	Hi	Hi	Med	Lo	V.Lo	V.Lo	Lo
Precip. Days	8	7	11	10	10	9	5	8	10	7	6	7	98
Precip. In.	1.2	1.2	2.6	3.5	4.3	5.6	4.4	3.8	4.2	3.2	1.5	1.5	37.0
Snowfall In.	6	4	4	1	0	0	0	0	0	0	1	4	20

ST. LOUIS — 568 ft.

	JAN	FEB	MAR	APR	MAY	JUN	JUL	AUG	SEP	OCT	NOV	DEC	ANN.
Av. High °F	40	44	53	67	76	85	88	87	80	70	54	43	66
Av. Low °F	23	26	34	46	56	65	69	67	59	48	36	27	46
Humidity	V.Lo	V.Lo	V.Lo	Lo	Med	Hi	Hi	Hi	Med	Lo	V.Lo	V.Lo	Lo
Precip. Days	8	8	11	11	11	9	9	7	9	8	8	10	109
Precip. In.	1.8	2.1	3.0	3.9	3.9	4.4	3.7	2.9	2.9	2.8	2.5	2.0	35.9
Snowfall In.	4	4	5	0	0	0	0	0	0	0	1	4	18

GREATEST U.S. MEASURED SNOW DEPTH: 451.0"
Tamarack, California — March 11, 1911

NEBRASKA

O M A H A — 978 ft.

	JAN	FEB	MAR	APR	MAY	JUN	JUL	AUG	SEP	OCT	NOV	DEC	ANN.
Av. High °F	33	39	48	64	74	83	89	87	79	69	51	38	63
Av. Low °F	12	17	26	40	52	61	66	64	54	43	29	18	40
Humidity	V.Lo	V.Lo	V.Lo	V.Lo	Lo	Hi	Hi	Hi	Med	Lo	V.Lo	V.Lo	Lo
Precip. Days	7	7	9	9	12	11	9	9	8	6	5	6	98
Precip. In.	.8	1.0	1.6	3.0	4.1	4.9	3.7	4.0	3.3	1.9	1.1	.8	30.2
Snowfall In.	8	7	7	1	<1	0	0	0	0	0	<1	6	32

NORTH DAKOTA

B I S M A R C K — 1,647 ft.

	JAN	FEB	MAR	APR	MAY	JUN	JUL	AUG	SEP	OCT	NOV	DEC	ANN.
Av. High °F	19	25	35	55	67	76	84	84	71	60	39	26	54
Av. Low °F	-3	2	15	31	42	52	57	55	44	33	18	5	29
Humidity	V.Lo	V.Lo	V.Lo	V.Lo	V.Lo	Med	Med	Med	Lo	V.Lo	V.Lo	V.Lo	V.Lo
Precip. Days	8	7	8	8	10	12	9	8	7	5	6	8	96
Precip. In.	.5	.4	.7	1.4	2.2	3.6	2.2	2.0	1.3	.8	.6	.5	16.2
Snowfall In.	7	6	8	4	1	0	0	0	<1	1	5	6	38

OHIO

C I N C I N N A T I — 761 ft.

	JAN	FEB	MAR	APR	MAY	JUN	JUL	AUG	SEP	OCT	NOV	DEC	ANN.
Av. High °F	40	43	52	66	75	84	87	86	80	69	53	42	65
Av. Low °F	24	26	34	45	54	63	66	64	57	47	36	27	45
Humidity	V.Lo	V.Lo	V.Lo	V.Lo	Med	Hi	Hi	Hi	Med	Lo	V.Lo	V.Lo	Lo
Precip. Days	12	11	13	12	12	13	10	9	9	9	10	11	131
Precip. In.	3.4	2.9	4.1	3.8	4.0	3.9	4.0	3.0	2.7	2.2	3.1	2.9	40.0
Snowfall In.	5	4	3	1	0	0	0	0	0	<1	2	4	19

C L E V E L A N D — 777 ft.

	JAN	FEB	MAR	APR	MAY	JUN	JUL	AUG	SEP	OCT	NOV	DEC	ANN.
Av. High °F	33	35	44	58	68	78	82	80	74	64	49	36	59
Av. Low °F	20	21	28	39	48	58	61	60	54	44	34	24	41
Humidity	V.Lo	V.Lo	V.Lo	V.Lo	Lo	Med	Hi	Hi	Med	Lo	V.Lo	V.Lo	Lo
Precip. Days	16	15	16	14	13	11	10	9	10	10	15	16	155
Precip. In.	2.5	2.2	3.0	3.5	3.5	3.3	3.4	3.0	2.8	2.6	2.8	2.4	35.0
Snowfall In.	11	11	10	2	<1	0	0	0	0	1	6	11	52

GREATEST U.S. SNOWFALL IN A SINGLE STORM: 189.0"
Mt. Shasta Ski Bowl, California — February 13 to 19, 1959

C O L U M B U S — 812 ft.

	JAN	FEB	MAR	APR	MAY	JUN	JUL	AUG	SEP	OCT	NOV	DEC	ANN.
Av. High °F	36	39	49	63	73	82	85	84	78	66	51	39	62
Av. Low °F	20	21	29	40	49	59	62	60	53	42	32	23	41
Humidity	V.Lo	V.Lo	V.Lo	Lo	Med	Med	Hi	Hi	Med	Lo	V.Lo	V.Lo	Lo
Precip. Days	13	12	14	13	13	11	11	9	9	8	11	12	136
Precip. In.	2.9	2.3	3.4	3.7	4.1	4.1	4.2	2.9	2.4	1.9	2.7	2.4	37.0
Snowfall In.	7	6	5	1	0	0	0	0	0	<1	3	6	28

OKLAHOMA

O K L A H O M A   C I T Y — 1,285 ft.

	JAN	FEB	MAR	APR	MAY	JUN	JUL	AUG	SEP	OCT	NOV	DEC	ANN.
Av. High °F	48	53	60	72	79	87	93	93	85	74	61	51	71
Av. Low °F	26	30	37	49	58	67	70	70	61	51	37	29	49
Humidity	V.Lo	V.Lo	V.Lo	Lo	Med	Hi	Hi	Hi	Med	Lo	V.Lo	V.Lo	Lo
Precip. Days	5	6	7	8	10	9	7	6	7	6	5	5	81
Precip. In.	1.1	1.3	2.0	3.5	5.2	4.2	2.7	2.6	3.5	2.6	1.4	1.3	31.4
Snowfall In.	3	2	2	0	0	0	0	0	0	0	<1	2	9

T U L S A — 650 ft.

	JAN	FEB	MAR	APR	MAY	JUN	JUL	AUG	SEP	OCT	NOV	DEC	ANN.
Av. High °F	47	52	60	72	79	87	93	93	85	75	61	51	71
Av. Low °F	26	30	37	50	58	67	71	70	62	51	38	30	49
Humidity	V.Lo	V.Lo	V.Lo	Lo	Med	Hi	Hi	Hi	Med	Lo	V.Lo	V.Lo	Lo
Precip. Days	6	7	8	9	10	9	7	7	7	7	6	7	90
Precip. In.	1.4	1.7	2.5	4.2	5.1	4.7	3.5	3.0	4.1	3.2	1.9	1.6	36.9
Snowfall In.	3	2	2	<1	0	0	0	0	0	0	2	1	10

SOUTH DAKOTA

R A P I D   C I T Y — 3,162 ft.

	JAN	FEB	MAR	APR	MAY	JUN	JUL	AUG	SEP	OCT	NOV	DEC	ANN.
Av. High °F	34	38	43	57	67	76	86	86	75	64	48	38	59
Av. Low °F	10	14	20	32	43	52	59	57	46	36	23	15	34
Humidity	V.Lo	V.Lo	V.Lo	V.Lo	V.Lo	Med	Med	Med	V.Lo	V.Lo	V.Lo	V.Lo	V.Lo
Precip. Days	7	8	9	10	12	13	9	7	6	4	6	6	97
Precip. In.	.5	.6	1.0	2.1	2.8	3.7	2.1	1.5	1.2	.9	.5	.4	17.1
Snowfall In.	5	6	9	6	1	<1	0	0	<1	2	4	5	39

GREATEST U.S. & NORTH AMERICAN SNOWFALL IN ONE SEASON: 1,122"
Mount Rainier — Paradise Ranger Station, Washington — 1971 to 1972

WISCONSIN

G R E E N   B A Y — 682 ft.

	JAN	FEB	MAR	APR	MAY	JUN	JUL	AUG	SEP	OCT	NOV	DEC	ANN.
Av. High °F	24	27	37	54	66	76	81	79	70	60	42	29	54
Av. Low °F	7	9	20	34	43	53	58	56	48	39	26	13	34
Humidity	V.Lo	V.Lo	V.Lo	V.Lo	Lo	Med	Hi	Med	Med	Lo	V.Lo	V.Lo	V.Lo
Precip. Days	10	8	11	11	12	11	10	10	10	8	9	11	121
Precip. In.	1.1	1.0	1.7	2.7	3.1	3.4	3.1	2.6	3.2	1.9	1.9	1.3	27.0
Snowfall In.	10	9	9	2	<1	0	0	0	0	<1	4	10	44

M I L W A U K E E — 672 ft.

	JAN	FEB	MAR	APR	MAY	JUN	JUL	AUG	SEP	OCT	NOV	DEC	ANN.
Av. High °F	27	30	39	55	65	75	80	80	72	61	44	32	55
Av. Low °F	11	15	23	35	43	54	59	59	51	41	29	17	36
Humidity	V.Lo	V.Lo	V.Lo	V.Lo	Lo	Med	Hi	Hi	Med	Lo	V.Lo	V.Lo	V.Lo
Precip. Days	11	9	12	12	11	9	11	9	9	8	10	11	123
Precip. In.	1.6	1.1	2.2	2.8	2.9	3.6	3.4	2.7	3.0	2.0	2.0	1.8	29.1
Snowfall In.	12	9	9	2	0	0	0	0	0	<1	3	10	45

GREATEST GLOBAL PRECIPITATION IN ONE HOUR: 12.00"
Holt, Missouri — June 22, 1947 (occurred in 42 minutes)

THE SOUTH

The climate of the South is warm, humid, and rainy. It can also be quite cloudy, even though it is part of the Sun Belt. It would be better to call it the "warmth belt," since it is usually warm for the greater part of the year.

The South isn't immune to cold, however. Subfreezing Canadian air masses sweep through the Midwest and head toward the South from the late fall through the spring months, and can drop temperatures into the teens all the way to the Gulf of Mexico and central Florida.

However, the air masses that normally dominate the southern states originate over the Gulf of Mexico or the warm waters of the Gulf Stream. This tepid "stream" starts off the southern tip of Florida, flows up the Atlantic seaboard, and can add quite a lot of moisture to the air masses affecting the southern states. As a result, southern humidities can be quite high, and thunderstorms a daily occurrence.

Because of the high moisture content of the air in the South, rainfall is often torrential, and lightning displays, loud thunder, and even tornadoes are common. But of all the storms of nature, perhaps none is as dramatic as the hurricane—and the South is the primary target for these huge, dramatic, and destructive storms.

The hurricane season begins in June and extends through October. No southern state is immune from the threat, either by a direct blow to its coast or by indirect threat from torrential rainfall, tornadoes, and strong winds as the hurricane moves inland and weakens. Most vulnerable to the effect of the hurricane winds and storm surge are the immediate shoreline and any structures or communities along that oceanfront.

Many major southern cities are in the "hurricane zone," including Brownsville, Corpus Christi, Galveston, New Orleans, Mobile, Tampa/St. Petersburg, Miami/West Palm Beach, Jacksonville, and Charleston, just to name some of the larger ones.

Hurricanes are more likely to affect the South in August and September, when water temperatures in the Gulf and Atlantic are at their warmest. The warmth of the water acts as the fuel that builds the hurricanes' clouds, lowers their pressure, and drives their winds into swirling furies.

The best month to visit the South is October. The fall is ideal if you want to avoid the bulk of the tornado and hurricane seasons and don't care for the heat and humidity of the summer or the chill of winter.

And if you want to avoid winter entirely, you can always spend it in Florida. The coldest weather usually stays north of a line that runs from Tampa to Daytona Beach. If you stay for the winter you'll be called a "snowbird." If you don't mind that, you'll have a wonderful time hearing about all the cold and snow up north while you bask in the sun.

ALABAMA

B I R M I N G H A M — 620 ft.

	JAN	FEB	MAR	APR	MAY	JUN	JUL	AUG	SEP	OCT	NOV	DEC	ANN.
Av. High °F	54	58	65	75	83	88	90	90	85	76	64	56	74
Av. Low °F	34	36	42	51	58	66	70	69	63	51	40	35	51
Humidity	V.Lo	V.Lo	Lo	Lo	Med	Hi	Hi	Hi	Hi	Med	Lo	V.Lo	Med
Precip. Days	11	11	11	9	9	10	13	10	8	6	9	11	118
Precip. In.	4.8	5.3	6.2	4.6	3.6	4.0	5.2	4.3	3.7	2.6	3.7	5.2	53.2
Snowfall In.	1	0	0	0	0	0	0	0	0	0	0	<1	1

ARKANSAS

L I T T L E   R O C K — 257 ft.

	JAN	FEB	MAR	APR	MAY	JUN	JUL	AUG	SEP	OCT	NOV	DEC	ANN.
Av. High °F	50	54	62	74	81	89	93	93	86	76	62	52	73
Av. Low °F	29	32	39	50	58	67	70	69	61	49	38	31	49
Humidity	V.Lo	V.Lo	V.Lo	Lo	Hi	Hi	V.Hi	Hi	Hi	Med	Lo	V.Lo	Med
Precip. Days	10	9	11	10	10	8	8	7	7	6	8	9	103
Precip. In.	4.3	4.4	4.9	5.3	5.3	3.5	3.4	3.0	3.6	3.0	3.7	4.1	48.5
Snowfall In.	2	1	1	0	0	0	0	0	0	0	<1	1	5

FLORIDA

D A Y T O N A   B E A C H — 31 ft.

	JAN	FEB	MAR	APR	MAY	JUN	JUL	AUG	SEP	OCT	NOV	DEC	ANN.
Av. High °F	69	70	75	80	85	88	90	90	87	81	75	70	80
Av. Low °F	48	49	53	59	65	70	72	73	72	65	55	49	61
Humidity	Med	Med	Med	Med	Hi	V.Hi	V.Hi	V.Hi	V.Hi	Hi	Med	Med	Hi
Precip. Days	7	8	8	6	9	13	14	14	13	11	7	7	117
Precip. In.	2.0	2.9	3.4	2.4	2.7	6.6	6.7	6.8	7.1	5.5	2.1	2.0	50.2
Snowfall In.	0	0	0	0	0	0	0	0	0	0	0	0	0

K E Y   W E S T — 4 ft.

	JAN	FEB	MAR	APR	MAY	JUN	JUL	AUG	SEP	OCT	NOV	DEC	ANN.
Av. High °F	75	76	79	82	85	88	89	89	88	84	80	76	83
Av. Low °F	65	66	69	72	76	78	79	79	78	76	71	67	73
Humidity	Hi	Hi	Hi	Hi	V.Hi	V.Hi	V.Hi	V.Hi	V.Hi	V.Hi	Hi	Hi	Hi
Precip. Days	6	6	5	4	8	11	12	15	15	11	7	7	107
Precip. In.	2.1	1.6	1.7	1.9	3.3	4.7	3.8	5.2	6.3	4.5	2.7	2.0	39.9
Snowfall In.	0	0	0	0	0	0	0	0	0	0	0	0	0

M I A M I — 25 ft.

	JAN	FEB	MAR	APR	MAY	JUN	JUL	AUG	SEP	OCT	NOV	DEC	ANN.
Av. High °F	76	77	80	83	85	88	89	90	88	85	80	77	83
Av. Low °F	59	59	63	67	71	74	76	76	75	71	65	60	68
Humidity	Med	Med	Hi	Hi	Hi	V.Hi	V.Hi	V.Hi	V.Hi	Hi	Hi	Med	Hi
Precip. Days	7	6	6	6	10	15	16	17	18	15	8	7	131
Precip. In.	2.2	2.0	2.1	3.6	6.1	9.0	6.9	6.7	8.7	8.2	2.7	1.6	59.8
Snowfall In.	0	0	0	0	0	0	0	0	0	0	0	0	0

O R L A N D O — 108 ft.

	JAN	FEB	MAR	APR	MAY	JUN	JUL	AUG	SEP	OCT	NOV	DEC	ANN.
Av. High °F	71	72	76	82	87	89	90	90	88	83	76	72	81
Av. Low °F	50	51	56	61	66	71	73	74	72	66	57	52	62
Humidity	Med	Med	Med	Med	Hi	V.Hi	V.Hi	V.Hi	V.Hi	Hi	Med	Med	Hi
Precip. Days	6	7	8	5	9	14	18	16	14	9	5	6	117
Precip. In.	2.3	2.9	3.5	2.7	2.9	7.1	8.3	6.7	7.2	4.1	1.6	1.9	51.2
Snowfall In.	0	0	0	0	0	0	0	0	0	0	0	0	0

T A M P A / S T.   P E T E R S B U R G — 19 ft.

	JAN	FEB	MAR	APR	MAY	JUN	JUL	AUG	SEP	OCT	NOV	DEC	ANN.
Av. High °F	71	72	75	82	88	90	90	90	89	84	77	72	82
Av. Low °F	50	52	56	62	67	72	74	74	73	66	56	51	63
Humidity	Med	Med	Med	Hi	Hi	V.Hi	V.Hi	V.Hi	V.Hi	Hi	Hi	Med	Hi
Precip. Days	6	7	7	5	6	12	16	16	13	7	5	6	106
Precip. In.	2.3	2.9	3.9	2.1	2.4	6.5	8.4	8.0	6.4	2.5	1.8	2.2	49.4
Snowfall In.	0	0	0	0	0	0	0	0	0	0	0	0	0

600 340 7

GEORGIA

ATLANTA — 1,054 ft.

	JAN	FEB	MAR	APR	MAY	JUN	JUL	AUG	SEP	OCT	NOV	DEC	ANN.
Av. High °F	51	55	61	71	79	85	87	86	81	73	62	53	70
Av. Low °F	33	36	41	51	59	67	69	69	63	52	41	34	51
Humidity	V.Lo	V.Lo	V.Lo	Lo	Med	Hi	Hi	Hi	Hi	Med	Lo	V.Lo	Med
Precip. Days	11	10	12	9	9	10	12	9	7	6	8	10	113
Precip. In.	4.3	4.4	5.8	4.6	3.7	3.8	4.9	3.5	3.2	2.5	3.4	4.2	48.3
Snowfall In.	1	<1	<1	0	0	0	0	0	0	0	0	<1	2

SAVANNAH (Hilton Head) — 46 ft.

	JAN	FEB	MAR	APR	MAY	JUN	JUL	AUG	SEP	OCT	NOV	DEC	ANN.
Av. High °F	60	63	70	78	84	89	91	90	86	78	70	62	77
Av. Low °F	38	41	47	54	62	69	72	72	68	57	46	40	55
Humidity	V.Lo	V.Lo	V.Lo	Med	Hi	Hi	V.Hi	V.Hi	Hi	Med	Lo	Lo	Med
Precip. Days	9	9	9	7	9	11	14	13	10	6	6	8	111
Precip. In.	3.3	3.2	3.8	3.1	4.2	5.5	6.8	7.0	5.0	2.5	2.0	2.8	49.2
Snowfall In.	T	T	T	0	0	0	0	0	0	0	T	T	T

KENTUCKY

LOUISVILLE — 477 ft.

	JAN	FEB	MAR	APR	MAY	JUN	JUL	AUG	SEP	OCT	NOV	DEC	ANN.
Av. High °F	42	45	54	67	76	84	87	87	81	70	55	44	66
Av. Low °F	25	27	34	45	54	63	66	65	58	46	35	27	45
Humidity	V.Lo	V.Lo	V.Lo	Lo	Med	Hi	Hi	Hi	Med	Lo	V.Lo	V.Lo	Lo
Precip. Days	12	11	13	12	11	10	11	8	8	7	10	11	124
Precip. In.	3.5	3.5	5.0	4.1	4.2	4.1	3.8	3.0	2.9	2.4	3.3	3.3	43.1
Snowfall In.	5	4	4	<1	0	0	0	0	0	<1	1	2	17

LOUISIANA

NEW ORLEANS — 8 ft.

	JAN	FEB	MAR	APR	MAY	JUN	JUL	AUG	SEP	OCT	NOV	DEC	ANN.
Av. High °F	62	65	70	78	85	90	90	91	87	80	70	64	78
Av. Low °F	44	46	51	59	65	71	73	73	70	60	50	45	59
Humidity	Lo	Lo	Med	Med	Hi	V.Hi	V.Hi	V.Hi	V.Hi	Hi	Med	Lo	Hi
Precip. Days	10	9	9	7	8	10	15	13	10	6	7	10	114
Precip. In.	4.5	4.8	5.5	4.2	4.2	4.7	6.7	5.2	5.6	2.3	3.9	5.1	56.8
Snowfall In.	0	0	0	0	0	0	0	0	0	0	0	0	0

MISSISSIPPI

J A C K S O N — 310 ft.

	JAN	FEB	MAR	APR	MAY	JUN	JUL	AUG	SEP	OCT	NOV	DEC	ANN.
Av. High °F	58	62	69	78	85	91	93	93	88	60	69	61	77
Av. Low °F	36	38	43	53	60	68	71	70	64	52	42	37	53
Humidity	Lo	Lo	Lo	Med	Med	Hi	V.Hi	V.Hi	Hi	Med	Lo	V.Lo	Med
Precip. Days	11	9	11	9	9	8	11	11	9	6	8	11	113
Precip. In.	4.5	4.6	5.6	4.7	4.4	3.4	4.3	3.6	3.0	2.2	3.9	5.0	49.2
Snowfall In.	<1	<1	<1	0	0	0	0	0	0	0	0	0	1

NORTH CAROLINA

C H A R L O T T E — 736 ft.

	JAN	FEB	MAR	APR	MAY	JUN	JUL	AUG	SEP	OCT	NOV	DEC	ANN.
Av. High °F	52	55	62	73	80	86	88	87	82	73	62	53	71
Av. Low °F	32	33	39	49	57	65	69	68	62	50	40	32	50
Humidity	V.Lo	V.Lo	V.Lo	Lo	Med	Hi	Hi	Hi	Hi	Med	V.Lo	V.Lo	Lo
Precip. Days	10	10	12	9	9	10	12	9	7	7	7	10	112
Precip. In.	3.5	3.8	4.5	3.4	2.9	3.7	4.6	4.0	3.5	2.7	2.7	3.4	42.7
Snowfall In.	2	1	1	0	0	0	0	0	0	0	<1	1	5

R A L E I G H — 434 ft.

	JAN	FEB	MAR	APR	MAY	JUN	JUL	AUG	SEP	OCT	NOV	DEC	ANN.
Av. High °F	51	53	61	72	79	86	88	87	82	72	62	52	70
Av. Low °F	30	31	37	47	55	63	67	66	60	48	38	31	48
Humidity	V.Lo	V.Lo	V.Lo	Lo	Med	Hi	Hi	Hi	Hi	Med	V.Lo	V.Lo	Lo
Precip. Days	10	10	11	9	10	9	11	10	8	7	8	9	112
Precip. In.	3.2	3.3	3.4	3.1	3.3	3.7	5.1	4.9	3.8	2.8	2.8	3.1	42.5
Snowfall In.	3	2	1	0	0	0	0	0	0	0	<1	1	7

SOUTH CAROLINA

C H A R L E S T O N — 9 ft.

	JAN	FEB	MAR	APR	MAY	JUN	JUL	AUG	SEP	OCT	NOV	DEC	ANN.
Av. High °F	60	62	68	76	83	88	89	89	85	77	68	61	75
Av. Low °F	37	39	45	53	61	68	71	71	66	55	44	38	54
Humidity	Lo	Lo	Lo	Med	Hi	Hi	V.Hi	V.Hi	Hi	Med	Lo	V.Lo	Med
Precip. Days	10	9	11	7	9	11	14	13	9	6	7	8	114
Precip. In.	2.9	3.3	4.8	3.0	3.8	6.3	8.2	6.4	5.2	3.0	2.1	3.1	52.1
Snowfall In.	<1	<1	<1	0	0	0	0	0	0	0	0	<1	1

LOWEST U.S. & NORTH AMERICAN
SEA LEVEL PRESSURE: 26.35"
Matecumbe Key, Florida — September 2, 1935

TENNESSEE

M E M P H I S — 258 ft.

	JAN	FEB	MAR	APR	MAY	JUN	JUL	AUG	SEP	OCT	NOV	DEC	ANN.
Av. High °F	49	53	61	73	81	89	92	91	84	75	62	52	72
Av. Low °F	32	34	41	52	61	69	72	70	63	51	40	34	52
Humidity	V.Lo	V.Lo	V.Lo	Lo	Med	Hi	Hi	Hi	Hi	Lo	V.Lo	V.Lo	Med
Precip. Days	10	10	11	10	9	8	9	8	7	6	8	10	106
Precip. In.	4.9	4.7	5.1	5.4	4.4	3.5	3.5	3.4	3.0	2.6	3.9	4.7	49.1
Snowfall In.	2	1	1	0	0	0	0	0	0	0	<1	1	5

N A S H V I L L E — 546 ft.

	JAN	FEB	MAR	APR	MAY	JUN	JUL	AUG	SEP	OCT	NOV	DEC	ANN.
Av. High °F	48	51	59	71	80	88	90	89	84	73	59	50	70
Av. Low °F	29	31	38	49	57	66	69	68	61	49	38	31	49
Humidity	V.Lo	V.Lo	V.Lo	Lo	Med	Hi	Hi	Hi	Hi	Lo	V.Lo	V.Lo	Lo
Precip. Days	11	11	12	11	11	10	10	9	8	7	9	11	120
Precip. In.	4.8	4.4	5.0	4.1	4.1	3.4	3.8	3.2	3.1	2.2	3.5	4.4	46.0
Snowfall In.	3	3	2	<1	0	0	0	0	0	0	1	2	11

TEXAS

A U S T I N — 597 ft.

	JAN	FEB	MAR	APR	MAY	JUN	JUL	AUG	SEP	OCT	NOV	DEC	ANN.
Av. High °F	60	64	71	79	85	92	95	96	89	81	70	63	79
Av. Low °F	39	43	48	58	65	71	74	74	69	59	48	42	57
Humidity	V.Lo	Lo	Lo	Med	Hi	Hi	Hi	Hi	Hi	Med	Lo	Lo	Med
Precip. Days	8	8	7	7	8	6	5	6	7	6	7	7	82
Precip. In.	1.9	3.1	1.9	3.5	4.0	3.1	1.9	2.2	3.7	3.0	2.0	2.2	32.5
Snowfall In.	1	<1	<1	0	0	0	0	0	0	0	0	0	1

D A L L A S / F T. W O R T H — 512 ft.

	JAN	FEB	MAR	APR	MAY	JUN	JUL	AUG	SEP	OCT	NOV	DEC	ANN.
Av. High °F	56	60	67	76	83	91	96	96	89	79	68	59	77
Av. Low °F	34	38	43	54	62	70	74	74	67	56	44	37	54
Humidity	V.Lo	V.Lo	Lo	Med	Hi	Hi	Hi	Hi	Hi	Med	Lo	V.Lo	Med
Precip. Days	7	6	7	9	8	6	5	5	7	6	6	6	78
Precip. In.	1.8	2.4	2.5	4.3	4.5	3.0	1.8	2.3	3.2	2.7	2.0	1.8	32.3
Snowfall In.	1	1	<1	0	0	0	0	0	0	0	<1	<1	3

H O U S T O N — 41 ft.

	JAN	FEB	MAR	APR	MAY	JUN	JUL	AUG	SEP	OCT	NOV	DEC	ANN.
Av. High °F	63	66	72	79	86	91	94	94	90	84	73	66	80
Av. Low °F	42	45	50	59	66	71	73	72	68	58	49	43	58
Humidity	Lo	Lo	Med	Hi	Hi	V.Hi	V.Hi	V.Hi	Hi	Hi	Med	Lo	Hi
Precip. Days	11	6	10	7	9	8	10	10	10	8	8	9	106
Precip. In.	3.6	3.5	2.7	3.5	5.1	4.5	4.1	4.4	4.7	4.1	4.0	4.0	48.2
Snowfall In.	<1	<1	0	0	0	0	0	0	0	0	0	0	<1

VIRGINIA

R I C H M O N D — 144 ft.

	JAN	FEB	MAR	APR	MAY	JUN	JUL	AUG	SEP	OCT	NOV	DEC	ANN.
Av. High °F	47	50	58	70	78	85	88	87	81	71	61	49	69
Av. Low °F	28	29	36	45	55	63	68	66	59	47	37	29	47
Humidity	V.Lo	V.Lo	V.Lo	Lo	Med	Hi	Hi	Hi	Hi	Lo	V.Lo	V.Lo	Lo
Precip. Days	10	9	11	9	11	10	11	10	8	7	8	9	113
Precip. In.	2.9	3.0	3.4	2.8	3.4	3.5	5.6	5.1	3.6	2.9	3.2	3.2	42.6
Snowfall In.	5	3	3	<1	0	0	0	0	0	0	<1	2	14

WEST VIRGINIA

C H A R L E S T O N — 939 ft.

	JAN	FEB	MAR	APR	MAY	JUN	JUL	AUG	SEP	OCT	NOV	DEC	ANN.
Av. High °F	44	46	55	68	77	83	86	84	79	69	56	45	66
Av. Low °F	25	27	34	44	52	61	64	63	56	45	35	27	44
Humidity	V.Lo	V.Lo	V.Lo	Lo	Med	Hi	Hi	Hi	Med	Lo	V.Lo	V.Lo	Lo
Precip. Days	15	14	15	14	13	11	13	10	9	9	12	14	149
Precip. In.	3.4	3.1	4.0	3.3	3.5	3.3	5.0	3.7	2.9	2.5	2.8	3.2	40.7
Snowfall In.	9	8	4	<1	0	0	0	0	0	<1	3	5	29

GREATEST U.S. & NORTH AMERICAN
PRECIPITATION IN 24 HOURS: 43.00"
Alvin, Texas — July 25 to 26, 1979

LOWEST GLOBAL PRECIPITATION IN ONE YEAR: 0.00"
Bagdad, CA (1913), Greenland Ranch, CA (1929),
Iquique, Chile (Nov '45–May '57)

THE WEST

The western United States offers some of the most diverse scenery and weather on earth. The dominant influence on the climate is the vast north Pacific Ocean. It's a cool body of water, and as a result the air masses that sweep over the West contain little of the oppressive humidity that covers the East and Midwest in the summer. But when these waters do give birth to storms in the winter, they are large and powerful, and can bring torrential rainfall and deep snows to the towering mountain ranges that run from Alaska to Mexico.

The immediate Pacific shoreline enjoys a mild, cool climate, thanks to the moderating influence of the ocean. In Washington, this shore is damp, rainy, and foggy. Off San Diego, it is still damp, but rainfall is infrequent and the temperatures are warmer. The fog is still a problem, especially in the spring and early summer. The fogs of San Francisco are world famous.

Farther inland, the climate becomes more extreme—that is, days are warmer, nights cooler, and the fog becomes more common in the winter than in the summer. If the ocean's cooling sea breezes are blocked by successive ranges of hills or mountains, the temperatures can soar to well over 100 during the summer months. California often reports the coolest and the hottest spots in the nation on many summer days. On a single day, Crescent City or Arcata can have a high of 58 with fog, while Death Valley can be 120 under a clear sky and blazing sun. That same morning, Truckee, high in the Sierra Nevada north of Lake Tahoe, might report a minimum temperature near freezing.

All of the factors that influence Western weather—distance from the ocean, elevation, and the effects of mountains and valleys as they block and channel air masses that attempt to flow over or into them—play their part in this scenario.

In the high, flat plateaus of the Western interior, rainfall becomes scarce, and the only thing that saves several states from being blazing deserts is the cooling effect of elevation.

The Rocky Mountains influence in many ways the air masses that pass over them—they intercept moisture from Pacific storms approaching from the west; they attempt to block cold, Canadian air masses in the winter, diverting them into the Midwest; they catch humidity flowing up over them from the south, southwest, or southeast, and generate massive thunderstorms in the summer; and they channel the jet stream winds that flow over them, generating fierce, warming, downslope winds (Chinook winds) on their eastern front.

Because of the tremendous diversity of western climates there really is no best time to visit—although as a general rule, late spring and early fall are almost ideal. Winters present problems of rain, fog, and snow. Summers present problems with heat and thunderstorms in some areas.

For the ideal conditions in any city you will be visiting, it's best to study the tables that follow. In the West, there's a climate to satisfy virtually everyone's needs.

ARIZONA

GRAND CANYON—6,971 ft.

	JAN	FEB	MAR	APR	MAY	JUN	JUL	AUG	SEP	OCT	NOV	DEC	ANN.
Av. High °F	41	45	50	60	70	81	85	82	77	65	51	43	63
Av. Low °F	20	21	25	31	39	46	54	53	47	37	27	21	35
Humidity	V.Lo	V.Lo	V.Lo	V.Lo	V.Lo	V.Lo	Lo	Lo	V.Lo	V.Lo	V.Lo	V.Lo	V.Lo
Precip. Days	6	6	6	5	3	3	11	11	6	5	5	6	74
Precip. In.	1.5	1.6	1.4	.9	.6	.4	1.9	2.3	1.6	1.2	.9	1.7	16.0
Snowfall In.	15	13	18	9	2	0	0	0	0	2	8	16	83

PHOENIX—1,083 ft.

	JAN	FEB	MAR	APR	MAY	JUN	JUL	AUG	SEP	OCT	NOV	DEC	ANN.
Av. High °F	65	69	75	84	93	102	105	102	98	88	75	66	85
Av. Low °F	38	41	45	52	60	68	78	76	69	57	45	39	55
Humidity	V.Lo	V.Lo	V.Lo	V.Lo	V.Lo	Lo	Med	Hi	Med	Lo	V.Lo	V.Lo	Lo
Precip. Days	3	4	3	2	1	1	4	5	3	3	2	4	35
Precip. In.	.7	.6	.8	.3	.1	.1	.8	1.2	.7	.5	.5	.8	7.1
Snowfall In.	0	0	0	0	0	0	0	0	0	0	0	0	0

CALIFORNIA

LAKE TAHOE — 6,230 ft.

	JAN	FEB	MAR	APR	MAY	JUN	JUL	AUG	SEP	OCT	NOV	DEC	ANN.
Av. High °F	36	38	43	51	60	68	79	78	70	58	45	39	55
Av. Low °F	17	18	22	27	31	38	43	43	38	32	25	21	30
Humidity	V.Lo	V.Lo	V.Lo	V.Lo	V.Lo	V.Lo	V.Lo	V.Lo	V.Lo	V.Lo	V.Lo	V.Lo	V.Lo
Precip. Days	11	10	10	7	5	3	1	1	3	5	6	9	71
Precip. In.	6.1	5.3	4.1	2.0	1.2	.6	.3	.1	.3	2.1	3.6	5.7	31.4
Snowfall In.	55	47	39	16	5	<1	0	0	<1	3	14	37	216

LOS ANGELES — 312 ft.

	JAN	FEB	MAR	APR	MAY	JUN	JUL	AUG	SEP	OCT	NOV	DEC	ANN.
Av. High °F	65	66	69	71	74	77	83	84	82	77	73	67	74
Av. Low °F	45	47	49	52	55	58	62	62	60	56	51	48	54
Humidity	Lo	Lo	Lo	Lo	Med	Med	Med	Med	Med	Med	Lo	Lo	Med
Precip. Days	6	6	5	4	1	1	1	0	1	2	3	5	35
Precip. In.	3.0	2.8	2.2	1.3	.1	.1	0	0	.2	.3	2.0	2.1	14.1
Snowfall In.	0	0	0	0	0	0	0	0	0	0	0	0	0

MONTEREY — 15 ft.

	JAN	FEB	MAR	APR	MAY	JUN	JUL	AUG	SEP	OCT	NOV	DEC	ANN.
Av. High °F	59	62	62	63	65	67	67	68	72	71	68	63	66
Av. Low °F	41	43	44	45	48	50	51	52	52	50	46	43	47
Humidity	Lo	Lo	Lo	Lo	Lo	Med	Med	Med	Med	Lo	Lo	Lo	Lo
Precip. Days	10	8	8	5	3	1	0	0	1	2	4	9	51
Precip. In.	3.5	2.7	3.0	1.3	.6	.1	0	0	.2	.7	1.6	3.1	16.8
Snowfall In.	0	0	0	0	0	0	0	0	0	0	0	0	0

PALM SPRINGS — 411 ft.

	JAN	FEB	MAR	APR	MAY	JUN	JUL	AUG	SEP	OCT	NOV	DEC	ANN.
Av. High °F	68	71	79	87	94	102	108	106	102	91	79	70	88
Av. Low °F	39	43	47	53	58	63	73	71	66	57	47	41	55
Humidity	V.Lo	V.Lo	V.Lo	V.Lo	Lo	Lo	Med	Med	Lo	Lo	V.Lo	V.Lo	Lo
Precip. Days	4	4	3	2	1	1	2	2	2	2	2	5	30
Precip. In.	1.2	1.3	.8	.3	0	0	.3	.3	.4	.3	.5	1.7	7.1
Snowfall In.	0	0	0	0	0	0	0	0	0	0	0	0	0

SACRAMENTO — 17 ft.

	JAN	FEB	MAR	APR	MAY	JUN	JUL	AUG	SEP	OCT	NOV	DEC	ANN.
Av. High °F	53	60	64	71	80	87	93	91	87	77	63	53	73
Av. Low °F	38	41	43	45	50	55	58	58	56	50	43	38	48
Humidity	V.Lo	Lo	Lo	Lo	Lo	Med	Med	Med	Med	Lo	Lo	Lo	Lo
Precip. Days	10	9	8	6	3	1	0	0	1	3	7	9	57
Precip. In.	3.7	2.7	2.2	1.5	.5	.1	0	.1	.2	1.0	2.1	3.1	17.2
Snowfall In.	0	0	0	0	0	0	0	0	0	0	0	0	0

SAN DIEGO — 19 ft.

	JAN	FEB	MAR	APR	MAY	JUN	JUL	AUG	SEP	OCT	NOV	DEC	ANN.
Av. High °F	64	65	67	68	70	72	76	77	76	73	71	66	72
Av. Low °F	46	48	50	53	57	60	63	64	62	57	51	47	55
Humidity	Lo	Lo	Lo	Med	Med	Med	Hi	Hi	Hi	Med	Lo	Lo	Med
Precip. Days	6	7	7	4	3	1	1	1	1	3	4	6	44
Precip. In.	1.9	1.9	1.5	.7	.3	.1	.1	.1	.1	.4	.9	1.9	9.9
Snowfall In.	0	0	0	0	0	0	0	0	0	0	0	0	0

SAN FRANCISCO — 52 ft.

	JAN	FEB	MAR	APR	MAY	JUN	JUL	AUG	SEP	OCT	NOV	DEC	ANN.
Av. High °F	56	59	61	63	65	69	69	70	72	69	64	57	65
Av. Low °F	40	43	44	45	48	50	52	52	52	49	45	42	47
Humidity	Lo	Lo	Lo	Lo	Lo	Med	Med	Med	Med	Med	Lo	Lo	Lo
Precip. Days	11	10	9	6	3	1	0	1	1	4	7	10	63
Precip. In.	4.4	3.0	2.5	1.6	.4	.1	0	0	.2	1.0	2.3	4.0	19.5
Snowfall In.	0	0	0	0	0	0	0	0	0	0	0	0	0

SANTA BARBARA — 120 ft.

	JAN	FEB	MAR	APR	MAY	JUN	JUL	AUG	SEP	OCT	NOV	DEC	ANN.
Av. High °F	65	65	68	70	72	73	77	78	78	76	73	67	72
Av. Low °F	39	42	44	47	50	52	56	56	55	50	44	42	45
Humidity	Lo	Lo	Lo	Lo	Lo	Med	Med	Med	Med	Med	Lo	Lo	Lo
Precip. Days	9	9	8	5	1	1	1	1	1	2	4	10	52
Precip. In.	3.6	3.8	3.1	1.2	.3	.1	.1	.1	.1	.6	1.2	4.0	18.2
Snowfall In.	0	0	0	0	0	0	0	0	0	0	0	0	0

SANTA MONICA — 14 ft.

	JAN	FEB	MAR	APR	MAY	JUN	JUL	AUG	SEP	OCT	NOV	DEC	ANN.
Av. High °F	65	65	66	68	70	72	75	76	75	72	69	66	70
Av. Low °F	46	47	48	51	54	57	56	60	59	55	51	48	53
Humidity	Lo	Lo	Lo	Lo	Med	Med	Hi	Hi	Med	Med	Lo	Lo	Med
Precip. Days	6	6	5	4	1	1	1	0	1	2	3	5	35
Precip. In.	2.2	2.7	2.5	.7	.1	0	0	0	.2	.3	1.1	3.1	12.9
Snowfall In.	0	0	0	0	0	0	0	0	0	0	0	0	0

YOSEMITE NATIONAL PARK — 3,985 ft.

	JAN	FEB	MAR	APR	MAY	JUN	JUL	AUG	SEP	OCT	NOV	DEC	ANN.
Av. High °F	47	52	59	67	73	80	90	90	83	71	58	47	68
Av. Low °F	26	28	31	37	43	47	54	52	47	39	31	28	39
Humidity	V.Lo	V.Lo	V.Lo	V.Lo	Lo	Lo	Med	Med	Lo	V.Lo	V.Lo	V.Lo	Lo
Precip. Days	11	10	10	7	5	3	1	1	3	5	6	9	71
Precip. In.	6.4	6.9	5.3	.2	1.4	.5	.2	.1	.4	2.0	3.8	7.4	34.6
Snowfall In.	16	13	16	9	0	0	0	0	0	0	4	15	73

COLORADO

A S P E N — 7,773 ft.

	JAN	FEB	MAR	APR	MAY	JUN	JUL	AUG	SEP	OCT	NOV	DEC	ANN.
Av. High °F	34	37	43	53	64	74	80	78	71	60	45	37	56
Av. Low °F	6	8	15	25	32	38	44	43	36	28	16	9	25
Humidity	V.Lo	V.Lo	V.Lo	V.Lo	V.Lo	V.Lo	Lo	Lo	V.Lo	V.Lo	V.Lo	V.Lo	V.Lo
Precip. Days	8	8	8	8	8	6	7	9	8	7	7	6	90
Precip. In.	1.8	1.8	1.8	1.7	1.6	1.1	1.5	1.6	1.4	1.4	1.4	1.5	18.6
Snowfall In.	27	25	24	11	3	0	0	0	1	5	17	21	134

D E N V E R — 5,280 ft.

	JAN	FEB	MAR	APR	MAY	JUN	JUL	AUG	SEP	OCT	NOV	DEC	ANN.
Av. High °F	44	46	50	61	70	80	87	86	78	67	53	46	64
Av. Low °F	16	19	24	34	44	52	59	57	48	37	25	19	36
Humidity	V.Lo	V.Lo	V.Lo	V.Lo	V.Lo	Lo	Lo	Lo	V.Lo	V.Lo	V.Lo	V.Lo	V.Lo
Precip. Days	6	6	9	9	10	9	9	8	6	5	5	5	87
Precip. In.	.6	.7	1.2	1.9	2.7	1.9	1.8	1.3	1.1	1.1	.8	.4	15.5
Snowfall In.	8	8	13	10	1	0	0	0	2	4	8	6	60

IDAHO

B O I S E — 2,844 ft.

	JAN	FEB	MAR	APR	MAY	JUN	JUL	AUG	SEP	OCT	NOV	DEC	ANN.
Av. High °F	37	44	52	61	71	78	91	88	78	65	49	39	63
Av. Low °F	21	27	31	37	44	51	59	57	49	39 -	31	25	39
Humidity	V.Lo	V.Lo	V.Lo	V.Lo	V.Lo	Lo	Lo	Lo	V.Lo	V.Lo	V.Lo	V.Lo	V.Lo
Precip. Days	12	10	9	8	8	7	2	3	4	6	10	12	91
Precip. In.	1.5	1.2	1.0	1.1	1.3	1.1	.1	.3	.4	.8	1.3	1.4	11.5
Snowfall In.	8	4	2	1	<1	0	0	0	0	<1	2	5	22

MONTANA

G R E A T F A L L S — 3,662 ft.

	JAN	FEB	MAR	APR	MAY	JUN	JUL	AUG	SEP	OCT	NOV	DEC	ANN.
Av. High °F	29	36	40	55	65	72	84	82	70	59	43	35	56
Av. Low °F	12	17	21	32	42	50	55	53	45	37	26	18	34
Humidity	V.Lo	V.Lo	V.Lo	V.Lo	V.Lo	Lo	Lo	Lo	V.Lo	V.Lo	V.Lo	V.Lo	V.Lo
Precip. Days	9	8	9	9	11	12	7	7	7	6	7	7	99
Precip. In.	.9	.7	1.0	1.2	2.4	3.1	1.3	1.1	1.2	.7	.8	.7	15.1
Snowfall In.	10	8	10	8	1	<1	0	0	1	3	7	9	57

NEVADA

LAS VEGAS — 2,006 ft.

	JAN	FEB	MAR	APR	MAY	JUN	JUL	AUG	SEP	OCT	NOV	DEC	ANN.
Av. High °F	56	61	68	78	88	97	104	102	95	81	66	57	79
Av. Low °F	33	37	42	50	59	67	75	73	65	53	41	34	52
Humidity	V.Lo	V.Lo	V.Lo	V.Lo	V.Lo	V.Lo	V.Lo	Lo	V.Lo	V.Lo	V.Lo	V.Lo	V.Lo
Precip. Days	3	2	3	2	1	1	3	3	2	2	2	2	26
Precip. In.	.5	.3	.3	.3	.1	.1	.4	.5	.3	.2	.4	.4	3.8
Snowfall In.	1	0	0	0	0	0	0	0	0	0	<1	<1	1

RENO — 4,397 ft.

	JAN	FEB	MAR	APR	MAY	JUN	JUL	AUG	SEP	OCT	NOV	DEC	ANN.
Av. High °F	45	51	56	64	72	80	91	89	82	70	56	46	67
Av. Low °F	18	23	25	30	37	43	47	45	39	31	24	20	32
Humidity	V.Lo	V.Lo	V.Lo	V.Lo	V.Lo	V.Lo	Lo	V.Lo	V.Lo	V.Lo	V.Lo	V.Lo	V.Lo
Precip. Days	6	6	6	4	5	3	3	2	2	3	5	6	51
Precip. In.	1.2	.9	.7	.5	.6	.4	.3	.2	.2	.4	.7	1.1	7.2
Snowfall In.	7	5	5	2	1	<1	0	0	0	<1	2	5	27

NEW MEXICO

ALBUQUERQUE — 5,311 ft.

	JAN	FEB	MAR	APR	MAY	JUN	JUL	AUG	SEP	OCT	NOV	DEC	ANN.
Av. High °F	47	53	59	70	80	90	92	90	83	72	57	48	70
Av. Low °F	24	27	32	41	51	60	65	63	57	45	32	25	44
Humidity	V.Lo	V.Lo	V.Lo	V.Lo	V.Lo	V.Lo	Lo	Med	Lo	V.Lo	V.Lo	V.Lo	V.Lo
Precip. Days	3	4	4	3	4	4	9	9	6	5	3	4	58
Precip. In.	.3	.4	.5	.5	.5	.5	1.4	1.3	.8	.8	.3	.5	7.8
Snowfall In.	2	2	2	1	0	0	0	0	0	0	1	3	11

SANTA FE — 6,344 ft.

	JAN	FEB	MAR	APR	MAY	JUN	JUL	AUG	SEP	OCT	NOV	DEC	ANN.
Av. High °F	43	48	54	64	74	84	87	84	81	68	52	45	65
Av. Low °F	19	22	26	34	44	53	58	56	50	39	24	19	37
Humidity	V.Lo	V.Lo	V.Lo	V.Lo	V.Lo	V.Lo	Med	Med	Lo	V.Lo	V.Lo	V.Lo	V.Lo
Precip. Days	2	2	2	1	2	2	5	6	2	2	1	1	27
Precip. In.	.5	.5	.5	.4	.9	.7	2.0	2.3	.6	.6	.3	.3	9.8
Snowfall In.	5	4	2	2	T	0	0	0	0	0	2	3	18.3

GREATEST U.S. & NORTH AMERICAN
SNOWFALL IN ONE MONTH: 390"
Tamarack (Elevation 8,000 ft.), California — January, 1911

OREGON

E U G E N E — 359 ft.

	JAN	FEB	MAR	APR	MAY	JUN	JUL	AUG	SEP	OCT	NOV	DEC	ANN.
Av. High °F	46	52	55	61	68	74	83	81	77	64	53	47	63
Av. Low °F	33	35	37	39	44	49	51	51	47	42	38	36	42
Humidity	V.Lo	V.Lo	V.Lo	Lo	Lo	Lo	Med	Med	Lo	Lo	Lo	V.Lo	Lo
Precip. Days	19	15	17	12	10	7	2	4	5	12	16	19	138
Precip. In.	7.5	4.7	4.4	2.3	2.1	1.3	.3	.6	1.3	4.0	6.5	7.6	42.6
Snowfall In.	5	<1	1	0	0	0	0	0	0	0	<1	1	8

P O R T L A N D — 154 ft.

	JAN	FEB	MAR	APR	MAY	JUN	JUL	AUG	SEP	OCT	NOV	DEC	ANN.
Av. High °F	44	50	54	60	67	72	79	78	74	63	52	46	62
Av. Low °F	33	36	37	41	46	52	55	55	51	45	39	35	44
Humidity	V.Lo	V.Lo	V.Lo	Lo	Lo	Med	Med	Med	Med	Lo	Lo	V.Lo	Lo
Precip. Days	19	16	17	14	12	9	4	5	7	13	17	19	152
Precip. In.	5.9	4.1	3.6	2.2	2.1	1.6	.5	.8	1.6	3.6	5.6	6.0	37.6
Snowfall In.	4	1	1	0	0	0	0	0	0	0	<1	1	7

UTAH

C E D A R   C I T Y — 5,622 ft.

	JAN	FEB	MAR	APR	MAY	JUN	JUL	AUG	SEP	OCT	NOV	DEC	ANN.
Av. High °F	42	45	52	62	71	81	87	85	78	66	53	44	64
Av. Low °F	19	23	28	35	43	52	60	58	50	38	27	20	38
Humidity	V.Lo	V.Lo	V.Lo	V.Lo	V.Lo	V.Lo	Lo	Lo	V.Lo	V.Lo	V.Lo	V.Lo	V.Lo
Precip. Days	3	3	3	3	2	1	3	3	2	3	2	3	31
Precip. In.	.9	1.0	1.3	1.1	.8	.5	1.2	1.2	.8	1.2	1.0	.9	11.7
Snowfall In.	8	7	8	3	1	0	0	0	0	1	4	5	35.5

S A L T   L A K E   C I T Y — 4,260 ft.

	JAN	FEB	MAR	APR	MAY	JUN	JUL	AUG	SEP	OCT	NOV	DEC	ANN.
Av. High °F	37	43	51	62	72	81	93	90	80	66	50	39	64
Av. Low °F	19	23	28	37	44	51	61	59	49	38	28	22	38
Humidity	V.Lo	V.Lo	V.Lo	V.Lo	V.Lo	Lo	Lo	Lo	V.Lo	V.Lo	V.Lo	V.Lo	V.Lo
Precip. Days	10	9	9	10	7	6	4	5	5	6	7	9	87
Precip. In.	1.3	1.2	1.6	2.1	1.5	1.3	.7	.9	.7	1.2	1.3	1.4	15.2
Snowfall In.	13	10	10	5	1	0	0	0	<1	1	6	12	58

HIGHEST GLOBAL AVERAGE ANNUAL RAINFALL: 460"
Mt. Waialeale, Kauai, Hawaii

WASHINGTON

S E A T T L E — 125 ft.

	JAN	FEB	MAR	APR	MAY	JUN	JUL	AUG	SEP	OCT	NOV	DEC	ANN.
Av. High °F	45	50	53	59	66	70	76	75	69	62	51	47	60
Av. Low °F	35	37	38	42	47	52	56	55	52	47	40	37	45
Humidity	V.Lo	V.Lo	V.Lo	V.Lo	Lo	Lo	Med	Med	Med	Lo	Lo	V.Lo	Lo
Precip. Days	20	16	17	14	10	9	5	6	8	10	18	20	153
Precip. In.	5.2	3.9	3.2	2.4	1.7	1.6	.9	.9	1.8	3.4	5.3	5.4	35.7
Snowfall In.	4	1	1	0	0	0	0	0	0	0	1	2	9

S P O K A N E — 2,357 ft.

	JAN	FEB	MAR	APR	MAY	JUN	JUL	AUG	SEP	OCT	NOV	DEC	ANN.
Av. High °F	31	39	46	57	67	74	84	82	73	58	42	34	57
Av. Low °F	20	25	29	35	43	49	55	54	47	38	29	24	37
Humidity	V.Lo	V.Lo	V.Lo	V.Lo	V.Lo	Lo	Lo	Lo	Lo	V.Lo	V.Lo	V.Lo	V.Lo
Precip. Days	15	12	11	9	9	8	4	5	6	8	12	16	115
Precip. In.	2.5	1.7	1.5	1.1	1.5	1.4	.4	.6	.8	1.4	2.2	2.4	17.5
Snowfall In.	19	8	5	1	<1	<1	0	0	0	1	5	15	53

W H I D B E Y   I S L A N D (San Juan Islands) — 46 ft.

	JAN	FEB	MAR	APR	MAY	JUN	JUL	AUG	SEP	OCT	NOV	DEC	ANN.
Av. High °F	45	49	51	55	60	63	66	67	64	57	50	46	56
Av. Low °F	35	36	38	41	46	50	52	52	49	44	39	36	43
Humidity	V.Lo	V.Lo	V.Lo	Lo	Lo	Lo	Med	Med	Med	Lo	V.Lo	V.Lo	Lo
Precip. Days	17	13	14	12	10	8	5	6	8	13	16	17	139
Precip. In.	2.4	1.7	1.6	1.5	1.2	1.2	.7	.9	1.2	1.8	2.5	2.6	19.3
Snowfall In.	3	1	1	T	T	0	0	0	0	T	T	2	7

WYOMING

Y E L L O W S T O N E   N A T I O N A L   P A R K — 6,239 ft.

	JAN	FEB	MAR	APR	MAY	JUN	JUL	AUG	SEP	OCT	NOV	DEC	ANN.
Av. High °F	26	29	36	48	58	67	77	76	65	52	38	28	50
Av. Low °F	10	10	17	26	34	41	46	45	37	29	20	12	27
Humidity	V.Lo	V.Lo	V.Lo	V.Lo	V.Lo	Lo	Lo	Lo	V.Lo	V.Lo	V.Lo	V.Lo	V.Lo
Precip. Days	13	11	12	10	13	12	10	9	8	9	10	12	129
Precip. In.	1.6	1.3	1.7	1.3	2.0	1.7	1.3	1.2	1.2	1.4	1.4	1.4	17.5
Snowfall In.	30	23	23	10	4	1	0	0	1	7	18	26	143

HIGHEST U.S. & NORTH AMERICAN TEMPERATURE: 134°F
Greenland Ranch, Death Valley, California — July 10, 1913

CHAPTER 2

Canada

Some people claim it's the most beautiful country on Earth. It has a larger population of moose than people. The country stretches from desolate polar wastelands in the north to fertile plains of wheat in the south. Its western shores are drenched with generous rains. Majestic mountain peaks divide the country into two very different landscapes. In the eastern provinces the lush farmland looks more like Northern Europe than America.

Because of their northern latitudes, all Canadian cities are cold in the winter—it's merely a matter of degree. British Columbia has the mildest weather. Daytime highs in Vancouver average low 40s in the winter and upper 60s to mid-70s in the summer. Rain can be almost a daily occurrence there from October through April. The driest and warmest month is July, but even then rain can fall once or twice a week.

East of the Rockies the climate is much more extreme. Winnipeg's highs average near 80 in the summer, and below 10 in the winter. Fortunately, oppressive humidity is rare. The best time to visit the wheat belt is in late summer.

The major cities of eastern Canada are warmer than the plains in the winter, but temperatures still average below freezing. Summers are warm and the humidity is moderate. The least rainy month in Toronto is August, with only nine wet days on average.

An ideal time to visit Canada—with warm temperatures, moderate humidity and low rainfall—is August.

CANADA

C A L G A R Y — 3,540 ft.

	JAN	FEB	MAR	APR	MAY	JUN	JUL	AUG	SEP	OCT	NOV	DEC	ANN.
Av. High °F	24	28	37	53	63	69	76	74	64	54	38	29	51
Av. Low °F	2	6	14	27	36	43	47	45	37	29	17	9	26
Humidity	V.Lo	V.Lo	V.Lo	V.Lo	V.Lo	Lo	Lo	Lo	V.Lo	V.Lo	V.Lo	V.Lo	V.Lo
Precip. Days	7	8	10	8	11	12	10	10	8	7	5	5	101
Precip. In.	.5	.5	.8	1.0	2.3	3.1	2.5	2.3	1.5	.7	.7	.6	16.7
Snowfall In.	5	5	8	6	5	1	0	0	3	4	7	6	50

E D M O N T O N — 2, 219 ft.

	JAN	FEB	MAR	APR	MAY	JUN	JUL	AUG	SEP	OCT	NOV	DEC	ANN.
Av. High °F	15	22	34	52	64	70	74	72	62	52	34	21	48
Av. Low °F	-4	1	12	28	38	45	49	47	38	30	16	5	25
Humidity	V.Lo	V.Lo	V.Lo	V.Lo	V.Lo	Lo	Med	Med	Lo	V.Lo	V.Lo	V.Lo	V.Lo
Precip. Days	12	9	10	8	12	15	14	12	9	9	11	12	133
Precip. In.	.9	.6	.8	.9	1.9	3.1	3.3	2.3	1.3	.7	.7	.8	17.3
Snowfall In.	9	7	7	5	2	0	0	0	1	4	8	8	51

M O N T R E A L — 187 ft.

	JAN	FEB	MAR	APR	MAY	JUN	JUL	AUG	SEP	OCT	NOV	DEC	ANN.
Av. High °F	21	23	33	50	64	74	78	75	67	54	39	26	50
Av. Low °F	6	8	19	33	47	57	61	59	51	40	27	13	35
Humidity	V.Lo	V.Lo	V.Lo	V.Lo	Lo	Med	Med	Med	Med	Lo	V.Lo	V.Lo	Lo
Precip. Days	15	14	14	12	12	13	12	11	12	13	14	15	157
Precip. In.	3.8	3.0	3.5	2.6	3.1	3.4	3.7	3.5	3.7	3.4	3.5	3.6	40.8
Snowfall In.	28	23	20	6	0	0	0	0	0	1	11	24	113

N I A G A R A   F A L L S — 324 ft.

	JAN	FEB	MAR	APR	MAY	JUN	JUL	AUG	SEP	OCT	NOV	DEC	ANN.
Av. High °F	30	32	39	56	66	76	81	79	71	61	47	35	56
Av. Low °F	18	19	25	37	45	56	61	60	52	43	33	23	39
Humidity	V.Lo	V.Lo	V.Lo	V.Lo	Lo	Med	Hi	Med	Med	Lo	V.Lo	V.Lo	V.Lo
Precip. Days	18	17	16	12	12	11	10	9	11	13	15	19	163
Precip. In.	3.0	2.8	2.9	3.0	3.1	1.7	2.3	4.5	2.7	2.6	2.6	2.9	34.1
Snowfall In.	19	16	11	2	0	0	0	0	0	0	7	15	70

O T T A W A — 339 ft.

	JAN	FEB	MAR	APR	MAY	JUN	JUL	AUG	SEP	OCT	NOV	DEC	ANN.
Av. High °F	21	22	33	51	66	76	81	77	68	54	39	24	51
Av. Low °F	3	3	16	31	44	54	58	55	48	37	26	9	32
Humidity	V.Lo	V.Lo	V.Lo	V.Lo	Lo	Med	Med	Med	Lo	V.Lo	V.Lo	V.Lo	V.Lo
Precip. Days	13	12	12	11	11	10	11	10	11	12	12	14	139
Precip. In.	2.9	2.2	2.8	2.7	2.5	3.5	3.4	2.6	3.2	2.9	3.0	2.6	34.3
Snowfall In.	22	17	14	5	0	0	0	0	0	1	6	17	82.0

QUEBEC — 296 ft.

	JAN	FEB	MAR	APR	MAY	JUN	JUL	AUG	SEP	OCT	NOV	DEC	ANN.
Av. High °F	18	20	31	45	61	72	76	73	64	51	36	22	47
Av. Low °F	2	4	15	29	41	52	57	54	47	37	24	9	31
Humidity	V.Lo	V.Lo	V.Lo	V.Lo	Lo	Med	Med	Med	Med	V.Lo	V.Lo	V.Lo	V.Lo
Precip. Days	14	14	14	12	13	14	13	12	13	13	14	17	163
Precip. In.	3.5	2.7	3.0	2.3	3.1	3.7	4.0	4.0	3.6	3.4	3.2	3.2	39.7
Snowfall In.	29	23	21	9	1	0	0	0	0	2	14	25	124

TORONTO — 379 ft.

	JAN	FEB	MAR	APR	MAY	JUN	JUL	AUG	SEP	OCT	NOV	DEC	ANN.
Av. High °F	30	30	37	50	63	73	79	77	69	56	43	33	53
Av. Low °F	16	15	23	34	44	54	59	58	51	40	31	21	37
Humidity	V.Lo	V.Lo	V.Lo	V.Lo	Lo	Med	Med	Med	Med	Lo	V.Lo	V.Lo	V.Lo
Precip. Days	16	12	13	12	13	11	10	9	12	11	13	13	145
Precip. In.	2.7	2.4	2.6	2.5	2.9	2.7	2.9	2.7	2.9	2.4	2.8	2.6	32.1
Snowfall In.	16	15	11	3	0	0	0	0	0	1	4	12	62

VANCOUVER — 45 ft.

	JAN	FEB	MAR	APR	MAY	JUN	JUL	AUG	SEP	OCT	NOV	DEC	ANN.
Av. High °F	41	44	50	58	64	69	74	73	65	57	48	43	57
Av. Low °F	32	34	37	40	46	52	54	54	49	44	39	35	43
Humidity	V.Lo	V.Lo	V.Lo	Lo	Lo	Med	Med	Med	Med	Lo	Lo	V.Lo	Lo
Precip. Days	20	17	17	14	12	11	7	8	9	16	19	22	172
Precip. In.	8.6	5.8	5.0	3.3	2.8	2.5	1.2	1.7	3.6	5.8	8.3	8.8	57.4
Snowfall In.	12	6	3	0	0	0	0	0	0	0	2	6	29

VICTORIA — 228 ft.

	JAN	FEB	MAR	APR	MAY	JUN	JUL	AUG	SEP	OCT	NOV	DEC	ANN.
Av. High °F	43	46	50	56	61	65	68	68	64	57	49	45	56
Av. Low °F	36	36	39	42	46	50	53	53	50	46	42	38	44
Humidity	V.Lo	V.Lo	V.Lo	Lo	Lo	Med	Med	Med	Med	Lo	Lo	V.Lo	Lo
Precip. Days	19	15	15	11	9	8	4	5	9	14	19	19	147
Precip. In.	4.5	3.0	2.3	1.2	1.0	.9	.4	.6	1.5	2.8	4.3	4.7	27.2
Snowfall In.	6	5	1	0	0	0	0	0	0	0	1	1	14

WINNIPEG — 786 ft.

	JAN	FEB	MAR	APR	MAY	JUN	JUL	AUG	SEP	OCT	NOV	DEC	ANN.
Av. High °F	7	12	27	48	65	74	79	76	65	51	30	15	47
Av. Low °F	-13	-9	5	27	39	50	55	51	43	31	13	-3	24
Humidity	V.Lo	V.Lo	V.Lo	V.Lo	V.Lo	Med	Med	Med	Lo	V.Lo	V.Lo	V.Lo	V.Lo
Precip. Days	12	11	9	9	10	12	10	10	9	6	9	11	138
Precip. In.	.9	.9	1.2	1.4	2.3	3.1	3.1	2.5	2.3	1.5	1.1	.9	21.2
Snowfall In.	9	8	10	4	1	0	0	0	0	3	9	9	53

HIGHEST CANADIAN TEMPERATURE: 113°F
Midale, Saskatchewan — July 5, 1937

CHAPTER 3

Mexico

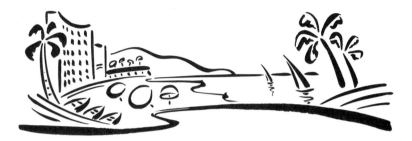

Mexico has a wide variety of climates that match its extreme geography. The country may be known for its lush tropical beach resorts, but most of the land is mountainous and includes some impressive volcanic peaks. The highest mountain can be found southeast of Mexico City. The volcano Popocatépetl soars to an impressive 17,883 feet above sea level—ten thousand feet higher than the city itself.

Mexico City has an unusual geographic setting. It lies in a high valley at an altitude of 7,575 feet and is surrounded by lofty, snow-capped peaks. Thanks to its altitude, temperatures in the city are mild despite its tropical latitude of 19 degrees north. The coolest month is January with a daytime average high of 66. The warmest month is May with highs in the upper 70s. Rainfall varies considerably, however, and by mid-summer it rains almost every day. Both July and August average 27 days of rain each. The best time to visit is in the early spring or late fall months when temperatures are warm and the rainfall infrequent. The best months are March, April, and November.

Mexico's tropical resorts have warm or hot weather and are humid all year long. The rain comes in a distinct season, and planning a trip around the rainfall is crucial. In Acapulco, Mazatlán, and Puerto Vallarta, very little rain falls from

November through April. The driest months are March and April. The rainy season begins in May and reaches a peak in September, when the days are steamy and heavy tropical downpours are the rule. In general, a trip to Mexico in the spring would find the best overall weather conditions.

Many of Mexico's largest cities and most popular travel destinations are in the interior at higher elevations, and enjoy pleasant, warm temperatures with a distinct rainy season during the summer months. For example, Guadalajara, at 5,005 feet, has high temperatures that range from the mid-70's during the winter to the upper 80's in the summer. Rainfall is highest from June through September, and very low during November through April—the best time to visit.

MEXICO

A C A P U L C O — 10 ft.

	JAN	FEB	MAR	APR	MAY	JUN	JUL	AUG	SEP	OCT	NOV	DEC	ANN.
Av. High °F	87	87	87	87	89	89	90	91	89	89	89	88	89
Av. Low °F	72	72	72	73	76	77	76	77	76	76	74	73	75
Humidity	Hi	Hi	Hi	Hi	V.Hi	V.Hi	V.Hi	V.Hi	V.Hi	V.Hi	V.Hi	Hi	V.Hi
Precip. Days	0	0	0	0	2	12	15	14	17	10	1	1	72
Precip. In.	.3	0	0	0	1.5	10.9	11.1	8.7	15.1	6.2	1.3	.4	55.5
Snowfall In.	0	0	0	0	0	0	0	0	0	0	0	0	0

C A N C U N — 16 ft.

	JAN	FEB	MAR	APR	MAY	JUN	JUL	AUG	SEP	OCT	NOV	DEC	ANN.
Av. High °F	81	82	84	85	88	89	90	90	89	87	84	82	86
Av. Low °F	67	68	71	73	77	78	78	77	76	74	72	69	74
Humidity	Hi	Hi	Hi	V.Hi	V.Hi	V.Hi	V.Hi	V.Hi	V.Hi	V.Hi	V.Hi	Hi	V.Hi
Precip. Days	5	4	3	2	4	6	4	4	7	8	5	6	58
Precip. In.	.8	1.3	1.0	1.0	2.5	3.5	2.5	2.8	4.5	7.0	7.0	1.3	35.2

C O Z U M E L — 15 ft.

	JAN	FEB	MAR	APR	MAY	JUN	JUL	AUG	SEP	OCT	NOV	DEC	ANN.
Av. High °F	82	84	85	87	86	87	87	89	97	96	93	82	85
Av. Low °F	68	68	68	72	73	74	74	74	74	73	71	68	71
Humidity	Hi	Hi	Hi	V.Hi	V.Hi	V.Hi	V.Hi	V.Hi	V.Hi	V.Hi	V.Hi	V.Hi	V.Hi
Precip. Days	10	14	5	10	13	19	11	10	20	6	5	5	128
Precip. In.	3.8	4.8	2.0	6.8	8.2	14.9	5.7	4.8	14.2	3.7	3.5	2.5	74.9

LOWEST NORTH AMERICAN
ANNUAL AVERAGE RAINFALL: 1.2"
Bataques, Mexico

GUADALAJARA — 5,005 ft.

	JAN	FEB	MAR	APR	MAY	JUN	JUL	AUG	SEP	OCT	NOV	DEC	ANN.
Av. High °F	75	78	82	86	89	86	80	81	80	80	79	76	81
Av. Low °F	44	45	49	53	57	62	62	62	61	56	48	45	54
Humidity	Lo	Lo	Lo	Lo	Lo	Med	Hi	Hi	Hi	Med	Lo	Lo	Med
Precip. Days	3	2	1	1	3	14	20	17	12	6	2	2	83
Precip. In.	.7	.2	.1	0	.7	7.6	10.0	7.9	7.0	2.1	.8	.8	37.9

LA PAZ — 85 ft.

	JAN	FEB	MAR	APR	MAY	JUN	JUL	AUG	SEP	OCT	NOV	DEC	ANN.
Av. High °F	74	77	81	86	89	94	96	95	94	90	83	77	86
Av. Low °F	54	55	56	58	61	66	73	75	75	68	63	58	64
Humidity	Med	Med	Med	Med	Hi	Hi	V.Hi	V.Hi	V.Hi	Hi	Hi	Med	Hi
Precip. Days	2	2	0	0	0	0	0	2	3	2	2	2	15
Precip. In.	.2	1.1	0	0	0	.2	.4	1.2	1.4	.6	.5	1.1	6.7

MAZATLÁN — 256 ft.

	JAN	FEB	MAR	APR	MAY	JUN	JUL	AUG	SEP	OCT	NOV	DEC	ANN.
Av. High °F	71	71	73	76	80	84	86	86	85	85	80	75	79
Av. Low °F	61	62	63	65	70	76	77	77	77	76	71	65	70
Humidity	Med	Med	Hi	Hi	Hi	V.Hi	V.Hi	V.Hi	V.Hi	V.Hi	Hi	Hi	Hi
Precip. Days	.8	1	.3	0	.1	4	14	15	14	4	2	2	57
Precip. In.	.2	.3	0	0	0	1.2	6.6	10.6	11.9	1.2	.7	.7	33.4

MEXICO CITY — 7,575 ft.

	JAN	FEB	MAR	APR	MAY	JUN	JUL	AUG	SEP	OCT	NOV	DEC	ANN.
Av. High °F	66	69	75	77	78	76	73	73	74	70	68	66	72
Av. Low °F	42	43	47	51	54	55	53	54	53	50	46	43	49
Humidity	V.Lo	V.Lo	V.Lo	Lo	Lo	Med	Med	Med	Med	Lo	Lo	V.Lo	Lo
Precip. Days	4	5	9	14	17	21	27	27	23	13	6	4	170
Precip. In.	.5	.2	.4	.8	2.1	4.7	6.7	6.0	5.1	2.0	.7	.3	29.4
Snowfall In.	0	0	0	0	0	0	0	0	0	0	0	0	0

PUERTO VALLARTA — 15 ft.

	JAN	FEB	MAR	APR	MAY	JUN	JUL	AUG	SEP	OCT	NOV	DEC	ANN.
Av. High °F	86	85	86	87	89	91	93	93	90	91	89	87	89
Av. Low °F	68	67	66	67	71	76	76	76	76	76	73	70	72
Humidity	Hi	Hi	Hi	Hi	Hi	V.Hi	V.Hi	V.Hi	V.Hi	V.Hi	V.Hi	Hi	V.Hi
Precip. Days	2	2	1	0	1	10	11	12	20	8	3	3	70
Precip. In.	.1	.2	0	0	.1	4.7	5.7	6.4	14.5	5.1	.9	1.8	39.5
Snowfall In.	0	0	0	0	0	0	0	0	0	0	0	0	0

LOWEST WESTERN HEMISPHERE
SEA LEVEL PRESSURE: 26.13"
*Near Mexico's Yucatán Peninsula in the eye of
Hurricane "Gilbert" — Sept. 13, 1988*

Part II

Europe
Africa
Middle East

CHAPTER 4

Europe

BRITISH ISLES

The warm Gulf Stream waters keep the British Isles warmer than their latitude would suggest. Most people correctly think of these islands as green, lush, cool, and damp. Rainfall in Ireland is spread uniformly through the year, thus giving the Emerald Isle its classic color. June is the driest of the summer months.

England is also sunniest in June. Temperatures during the afternoon average near 70 until September. Rain falls on average two to three times a week all year so it's a good idea to expect it. Scotland has a similar rainfall pattern, but it's a bit cooler than England. Again, the best month for sunshine and mild temperatures is June.

ENGLAND

L O N D O N — 149 ft.

	JAN	FEB	MAR	APR	MAY	JUN	JUL	AUG	SEP	OCT	NOV	DEC	ANN.
Av. High °F	44	45	51	56	63	69	73	72	67	58	49	45	58
Av. Low °F	35	35	37	40	45	51	55	54	51	44	39	36	43
Humidity	V.Lo	V.Lo	V.Lo	V.Lo	Lo	Med	Med	Med	Med	Lo	Lo	V.Lo	Lo
Precip. Days	17	13	11	14	13	11	13	13	13	14	16	16	164
Precip. In.	2.0	1.5	1.4	1.8	1.8	1.6	2.0	2.2	1.8	2.3	2.5	2.0	22.9
Snowfall In.	2	1	0	0	0	0	0	0	0	0	0	1	4

IRELAND

D U B L I N — 155 ft.

	JAN	FEB	MAR	APR	MAY	JUN	JUL	AUG	SEP	OCT	NOV	DEC	ANN.
Av. High °F	47	47	51	54	59	65	67	67	63	57	51	47	56
Av. Low °F	35	35	36	38	42	48	51	51	47	43	38	36	42
Humidity	V.Lo	V.Lo	V.Lo	V.Lo	Lo	Lo	Med	Med	Med	Lo	Lo	Lo	Lo
Precip. Days	13	11	10	11	11	11	13	13	12	12	12	13	142
Precip. In.	2.7	2.2	2.0	1.9	2.3	2.0	2.8	3.0	2.8	2.7	2.7	2.6	29.7
Snowfall In.	2	3	1	0	0	0	0	0	0	0	1	1	6

NORTHERN IRELAND

B E L F A S T — 24 ft.

	JAN	FEB	MAR	APR	MAY	JUN	JUL	AUG	SEP	OCT	NOV	DEC	ANN.
Av. High °F	43	44	49	53	59	63	65	65	61	55	48	45	54
Av. Low °F	35	35	37	39	43	48	52	51	49	44	39	37	42
Humidity	V.Lo	V.Lo	V.Lo	Lo	Lo	Med	Med	Med	Med	Lo	Lo	Lo	Lo
Precip. Days	20	17	16	15	15	16	19	18	18	19	19	21	213
Precip. In.	4.1	2.8	2.4	2.4	2.5	2.4	3.4	3.5	3.3	3.9	3.6	3.9	38.2
Snowfall In.	7	6	4	1	0	0	0	0	0	0	1	4	23

SCOTLAND

G L A S G O W — 29 ft.

	JAN	FEB	MAR	APR	MAY	JUN	JUL	AUG	SEP	OCT	NOV	DEC	ANN.
Av. High °F	43	44	48	53	59	64	66	65	61	54	47	43	54
Av. Low °F	34	35	36	38	42	47	52	51	47	43	37	36	41
Humidity	V.Lo	V.Lo	V.Lo	Lo	Lo	Med	Med	Med	Med	Lo	Lo	V.Lo	Lo
Precip. Days	21	17	15	15	15	15	17	18	17	19	19	20	208
Precip. In.	4.7	3.1	2.5	2.5	2.6	2.4	3.2	3.5	3.7	4.7	4.0	4.1	41.0
Snowfall In.	9	6	2	1	0	0	0	0	0	1	4	7	30

CENTRAL EUROPE

Most of western France, the Low Countries, and northern Germany have a similar climate, especially during the prime travel months. Temperatures reach the 70s during summer afternoons, and nights are cool. Rain falls two or three times a week, but is less common in June and September. If you're looking for mild temperatures, long days, and the lowest chance of rainfall, June is the best month to visit the continent. Months to be avoided would be November through March—unless you want to go skiing in the Alps.

The broad, low central European plain is broken by towering mountain ranges that create an entirely new climate of their own. Eastern and southern France, southern Germany, Austria, Switzerland, northern Italy, and the Czech Republic are hilly or mountainous—so the climate here is as diverse as the geography.

The climate of Munich, in southern Germany (gateway to the Alps), is wetter than the lowlands farther north. Here, it rains more in June and July than in any other months of the year. However, the region has such beauty that even an occasional wet day won't be too much of a disappointment.

Geneva, Switzerland, has a lull in the rain during July—the best of its summer months. Zurich is wetter than Geneva, averaging 15 days of rainfall in July. Summer afternoons are warm with temperatures in the upper 70s. By September the rains ease off to one day in three, and highs average near 70. Vienna is mild from May through September with rain falling every third day. August is the wettest summer month in this gorgeous Alpine city.

AUSTRIA

VIENNA — 664 ft.

	JAN	FEB	MAR	APR	MAY	JUN	JUL	AUG	SEP	OCT	NOV	DEC	ANN.
Av. High °F	34	38	47	57	66	71	75	73	66	55	44	37	55
Av. Low °F	26	28	34	41	50	56	59	58	52	44	36	30	43
Humidity	V.Lo	V.Lo	V.Lo	Lo	Lo	Med	Med	Med	Med	Lo	V.Lo	V.Lo	Lo
Precip. Days	8	7	7	9	9	9	9	10	7	8	8	9	100
Precip. In.	1.5	1.4	1.8	2.0	2.8	2.7	3.0	2.7	2.0	2.0	1.9	1.8	25.6
Snowfall In.	13	10	2	0	0	0	0	0	0	1	0	4	30

BELGIUM

BRUSSELS — 328 ft.

	JAN	FEB	MAR	APR	MAY	JUN	JUL	AUG	SEP	OCT	NOV	DEC	ANN.
Av. High °F	42	43	49	56	65	70	73	72	67	58	47	42	57
Av. Low °F	31	31	35	39	46	50	54	54	50	44	36	33	42
Humidity	V.Lo	V.Lo	V.Lo	Lo	Lo	Med	Med	Med	Med	Lo	V.Lo	V.Lo	Lo
Precip. Days	12	10	11	12	10	11	11	11	10	12	12	13	135
Precip. In.	2.6	2.0	2.4	2.5	2.5	2.6	3.5	3.0	2.6	3.0	3.1	3.2	33.0
Snowfall In.	4	3	1	0	0	0	0	0	0	0	2	5	15

FRANCE

P A R I S — 164 ft.

	JAN	FEB	MAR	APR	MAY	JUN	JUL	AUG	SEP	OCT	NOV	DEC	ANN.
Av. High °F	42	45	52	60	67	73	76	75	69	59	49	43	59
Av. Low °F	32	33	36	41	47	52	55	55	50	44	38	33	43
Humidity	V.Lo	V.Lo	V.Lo	Lo	Lo	Med	Med	Med	Med	Lo	Lo	V.Lo	Lo
Precip. Days	15	13	15	14	13	11	12	12	11	14	15	17	162
Precip. In.	1.5	1.3	1.5	1.7	2.0	2.1	2.1	2.0	2.0	2.2	2.0	1.9	22.3
Snowfall In.	4	3	1	0	0	0	0	0	0	0	1	3	11

GERMANY

B E R L I N — 187 ft.

	JAN	FEB	MAR	APR	MAY	JUN	JUL	AUG	SEP	OCT	NOV	DEC	ANN.
Av. High °F	35	38	46	55	65	70	74	72	66	55	43	37	55
Av. Low °F	26	27	32	38	46	51	55	54	48	41	33	29	40
Humidity	V.Lo	V.Lo	V.Lo	V.Lo	Lo	Med	Med	Med	Lo	Lo	V.Lo	V.Lo	Lo
Precip. Days	10	8	9	9	8	9	10	10	8	8	8	11	108
Precip. In.	1.9	1.3	1.5	1.7	1.9	2.3	3.1	2.2	1.9	1.7	1.7	1.9	23.1
Snowfall In.	5	6	1	0	0	0	0	0	0	0	2	1	15

F R A N K F U R T — 338 ft.

	JAN	FEB	MAR	APR	MAY	JUN	JUL	AUG	SEP	OCT	NOV	DEC	ANN.
Av. High °F	37	42	49	58	67	72	75	74	67	56	45	39	57
Av. Low °F	29	31	35	41	48	53	56	55	51	43	36	31	42
Humidity	V.Lo	V.Lo	V.Lo	Lo	Lo	Med	Med	Med	Med	Lo	V.Lo	V.Lo	Lo
Precip. Days	9	9	9	9	9	9	10	10	9	9	9	11	112
Precip. In.	1.7	1.3	1.6	1.5	2.0	2.5	2.8	2.6	1.9	2.2	2.0	2.0	24.1
Snowfall In.	7	5	2	<1	0	0	0	0	0	<1	6	11	37

M U N I C H — 1,739 ft.

	JAN	FEB	MAR	APR	MAY	JUN	JUL	AUG	SEP	OCT	NOV	DEC	ANN.
Av. High °F	33	37	45	54	63	69	72	71	64	53	42	36	53
Av. Low °F	23	25	31	37	45	51	54	53	48	40	31	26	39
Humidity	V.Lo	V.Lo	V.Lo	V.Lo	Lo	Med	Med	Med	Med	Lo	V.Lo	V.Lo	Lo
Precip. Days	10	9	10	13	13	14	14	13	11	10	9	11	137
Precip. In.	1.7	1.4	1.9	2.7	3.7	4.6	4.7	4.2	3.2	2.2	1.9	1.9	34.1
Snowfall In.	12	11	3	2	1	0	0	0	0	2	3	10	44

NETHERLANDS

AMSTERDAM — 5 ft.

	JAN	FEB	MAR	APR	MAY	JUN	JUL	AUG	SEP	OCT	NOV	DEC	ANN.
Av. High °F	40	41	46	52	60	65	69	68	64	56	47	41	54
Av. Low °F	34	34	37	43	50	55	59	59	56	48	41	35	46
Humidity	V.Lo	V.Lo	V.Lo	Lo	Med	Med	Med	Med	Med	Lo	Lo	V.Lo	Lo
Precip. Days	19	15	13	14	12	12	14	14	15	18	19	19	184
Precip. In.	2.0	1.4	1.3	1.6	1.8	1.8	2.6	2.7	2.8	2.8	2.6	2.2	25.6
Snowfall In.	4	4	3	1	0	0	0	0	0	0	1	4	17

SWITZERLAND

GENEVA — 1,329 ft.

	JAN	FEB	MAR	APR	MAY	JUN	JUL	AUG	SEP	OCT	NOV	DEC	ANN.
Av. High °F	39	43	51	58	66	73	77	76	69	58	47	40	58
Av. Low °F	29	30	35	41	48	55	58	57	52	44	37	31	43
Humidity	V.Lo	V.Lo	V.Lo	V.Lo	Lo	Med	Med	Med	Med	Lo	V.Lo	V.Lo	Lo
Precip. Days	10	9	10	11	12	11	9	10	10	11	11	10	124
Precip. In.	1.9	1.8	2.2	2.5	3.0	3.1	2.9	3.6	3.6	3.8	3.1	2.4	33.9
Snowfall In.	10	7	2	1	0	0	0	0	0	1	4	7	30

ZURICH — 1,617 ft.

	JAN	FEB	MAR	APR	MAY	JUN	JUL	AUG	SEP	OCT	NOV	DEC	ANN.
Av. High °F	36	41	52	60	67	73	77	76	70	57	46	36	58
Av. Low °F	26	29	34	41	47	53	56	56	52	43	36	29	42
Humidity	V.Lo	V.Lo	V.Lo	V.Lo	Lo	Lo	Med	Med	Med	Lo	V.Lo	V.Lo	Lo
Precip. Days	10	8	9	12	13	15	14	13	11	11	10	10	136
Precip. In.	1.9	2.2	3.0	3.8	4.5	5.3	5.2	5.2	4.3	4.1	2.8	2.9	45.2
Snowfall In.	15	11	2	0	0	0	0	0	0	<1	18	26	72

EASTERN EUROPE

The best time to visit Eastern Europe is during the late spring through early fall. Temperatures are pleasantly warm during the days, and the nights are mild. The countryside is kept green by occasional rainy days, and humidity is comfortable even during the summer. Winters can be quite cold as all of Eastern Europe falls under the grip of severe cold waves.

BOSNIA AND HERZEGOVINA

S A R A J E V O — 2,067 ft.

	JAN	FEB	MAR	APR	MAY	JUN	JUL	AUG	SEP	OCT	NOV	DEC	ANN.
Av. High °F	37	42	51	62	69	75	80	81	75	60	50	41	60
Av. Low °F	24	27	33	40	47	53	56	56	51	42	36	29	41
Humidity	V.Lo	V.Lo	V.Lo	V.Lo	Lo	Med	Med	Med	Lo	Lo	V.Lo	V.Lo	Lo
Precip. Days	9	10	9	9	12	10	8	7	6	10	10	10	110
Precip. In.	2.5	2.8	2.1	1.9	3.4	3.3	2.4	2.3	2.6	3.6	3.7	3.5	34.1
Snowfall In.	25	23	13	5	1	0	0	0	0	3	17	22	109

CZECH REPUBLIC

P R A G U E — 702 ft.

	JAN	FEB	MAR	APR	MAY	JUN	JUL	AUG	SEP	OCT	NOV	DEC	ANN.
Av. High °F	34	38	45	55	65	72	74	73	65	54	41	34	54
Av. Low °F	25	28	33	40	49	55	58	57	52	44	35	29	42
Humidity	V.Lo	V.Lo	V.Lo	V.Lo	Lo	Med	Med	Med	Lo	Lo	V.Lo	V.Lo	Lo
Precip. Days	12	11	13	12	13	14	14	12	11	11	12	13	148
Precip. In.	.9	.8	1.1	1.5	2.4	2.8	2.6	2.2	1.7	1.2	1.2	.9	19.3
Snowfall In.	7	6	3	1	0	0	0	0	0	2	7	7	32

HUNGARY

B U D A P E S T — 394 ft.

	JAN	FEB	MAR	APR	MAY	JUN	JUL	AUG	SEP	OCT	NOV	DEC	ANN.
Av. High °F	35	40	51	62	72	78	82	81	74	61	47	38	60
Av. Low °F	26	28	36	44	52	57	61	59	53	45	37	31	44
Humidity	V.Lo	V.Lo	V.Lo	V.Lo	Lo	Med	Med	Med	Med	Lo	V.Lo	V.Lo	Lo
Precip. Days	7	6	7	8	9	8	7	6	7	8	8	9	90
Precip. In.	1.5	1.5	1.7	2.0	2.7	2.6	2.0	1.9	1.8	2.1	2.4	2.0	24.2
Snowfall In.	5	5	1	0	0	0	0	0	0	0	2	5	15

POLAND

W A R S A W — 394 ft.

	JAN	FEB	MAR	APR	MAY	JUN	JUL	AUG	SEP	OCT	NOV	DEC	ANN.
Av. High °F	30	32	41	54	67	72	75	73	65	54	40	32	53
Av. Low °F	21	23	28	38	48	53	56	55	48	41	32	25	39
Humidity	V.Lo	V.Lo	V.Lo	V.Lo	Lo	Med	Med	Med	Lo	Lo	V.Lo	V.Lo	V.Lo
Precip. Days	8	7	6	8	8	11	11	11	9	10	7	8	104
Precip. In.	1.2	1.1	1.3	1.5	1.9	2.6	3.0	3.0	1.9	1.7	1.4	1.4	22.0
Snowfall In.	11	9	4	1	0	0	0	0	0	1	5	9	40

ITALY AND GREECE

While these two countries, both rich in history, are thought of as generally sunny and warm, there *are* important differences in climate that can affect your travel plans. Italy gets more rain than Greece. It rains in Rome an average of 76 days a year, and only 48 days in Athens. Rome has higher summer humidity. In the winter, their climates are almost the same.

The best time to visit Rome is in June. July and August are very warm and muggy. By September and October the rain increases.

If you are headed for Athens, the best months are May, June, September, and October (particularly May). By October, the rains return, but only one day a week on average. Midsummer can be hot during the day with temperatures near 90 and uncomfortable humidity levels. Nights are warm with temperatures hovering in the 70s. Nights are cooler and more comfortable in May and October.

ITALY

FLORENCE — 144 ft.

	JAN	FEB	MAR	APR	MAY	JUN	JUL	AUG	SEP	OCT	NOV	DEC	ANN.
Av. High °F	49	53	60	68	75	84	89	88	81	69	58	50	69
Av. Low °F	35	36	40	46	53	58	63	62	58	51	42	37	49
Humidity	V.Lo	V.Lo	Lo	Lo	Med	Hi	Hi	Hi	Med	Med	Lo	V.Lo	Lo
Precip. Days	9	9	7	7	9	5	4	4	6	9	10	9	88
Precip. In.	3.6	4.0	2.1	2.5	2.7	2.0	1.3	1.2	3.7	5.1	4.6	3.4	36.2
Snowfall In.	T	T	0	0	0	0	0	0	0	0	0	T	T

NAPLES — 220 ft.

	JAN	FEB	MAR	APR	MAY	JUN	JUL	AUG	SEP	OCT	NOV	DEC	ANN.
Av. High °F	54	55	60	67	73	81	86	86	81	72	63	57	70
Av. Low °F	40	41	45	49	56	62	66	66	62	55	48	43	53
Humidity	V.Lo	V.Lo	Lo	Lo	Med	Med	Hi	Hi	Hi	Med	Lo	V.Lo	Lo
Precip. Days	11	11	6	6	6	3	1	3	6	9	11	11	84
Precip. In.	4.8	3.5	1.7	1.8	2.2	.7	.6	1.3	4.3	4.6	4.1	4.7	34.3
Snowfall In.	1	0	0	0	0	0	0	0	0	0	0	0	1

ROME — 377 ft.

	JAN	FEB	MAR	APR	MAY	JUN	JUL	AUG	SEP	OCT	NOV	DEC	ANN.
Av. High °F	54	56	62	68	74	82	88	88	83	73	63	56	71
Av. Low °F	39	39	42	46	55	60	64	64	61	53	46	41	51
Humidity	V.Lo	V.Lo	Lo	Lo	Med	Med	Hi	Hi	Med	Med	Lo	Lo	Med
Precip. Days	8	11	5	6	6	3	2	3	6	9	8	9	76
Precip. In.	2.7	2.3	1.5	1.7	2.0	1.0	.6	.9	2.7	3.7	3.8	2.8	25.7
Snowfall In.	1	<1	0	0	0	0	0	0	0	0	0	<1	2

VENICE — 13 ft.

	JAN	FEB	MAR	APR	MAY	JUN	JUL	AUG	SEP	OCT	NOV	DEC	ANN.
Av. High °F	43	46	54	63	71	78	82	82	78	65	54	46	63
Av. Low °F	33	35	41	49	57	64	67	67	62	52	43	37	51
Humidity	V.Lo	V.Lo	V.Lo	Lo	Med	Hi	Hi	Hi	Hi	Med	Lo	V.Lo	Lo
Precip. Days	6	5	6	5	8	8	8	5	5	7	7	7	77
Precip. In.	1.6	1.8	2.0	1.6	3.2	2.6	2.8	1.7	2.4	3.4	3.1	2.4	28.6
Snowfall In.	2	2	<1	0	0	0	0	0	0	0	<1	1	6

GREECE

ATHENS — 351 ft.

	JAN	FEB	MAR	APR	MAY	JUN	JUL	AUG	SEP	OCT	NOV	DEC	ANN.
Av. High °F	54	55	60	67	77	85	90	90	83	74	64	57	71
Av. Low °F	42	43	46	52	60	67	72	72	66	60	52	46	57
Humidity	V.Lo	Lo	V.Lo	Lo	Med	Med	Med	Med	Med	Med	Med	Lo	Lo
Precip. Days	7	6	5	3	3	2	.7	.9	2	4	6	7	47
Precip. In.	2.2	1.6	1.4	.8	.8	.6	.2	.4	.6	1.7	2.8	2.8	15.8
Snowfall In.	1	<1	0	0	0	0	0	0	0	0	0	<1	2

THE RIVIERA

The Riviera enjoys warm, humid summers and cool, showery winters. The warm waters of the Mediterranean often make afternoon weather along the entire coastline uncomfortably muggy. It can also rain in the summer—the driest month is July. Rainfall peaks in the winter, when temperatures are in the cool 50s during the day (much like Northern California). Best months to visit are May through October. For the ideal combination of moderate temperature, humidity, and rainfall, June would make an excellent choice.

FRANCE

N I C E — 39 ft.

	JAN	FEB	MAR	APR	MAY	JUN	JUL	AUG	SEP	OCT	NOV	DEC	ANN.
Av. High °F	56	56	59	64	69	76	81	81	77	70	62	58	67
Av. Low °F	40	41	45	49	56	62	66	66	62	55	48	43	53
Humidity	V.Lo	V.Lo	Lo	Lo	Med	Med	Hi	Hi	Hi	Med	Lo	V.Lo	Lo
Precip. Days	8	8	8	7	8	5	2	5	6	9	7	8	81
Precip. In.	2.4	2.4	3.2	1.9	2.8	1.0	.7	1.3	3.0	4.5	5.6	3.5	32.3
Snowfall In.	0	0	0	0	0	0	0	0	0	0	0	0	0

RUSSIA

The best time to visit Russia is the summer. It's simply too cold to really enjoy your trip at any other time of the year—unless you are visiting to see how people cope with the chilly temperatures!

Summer is the rainiest time of the year, averaging one or two days of rain per week. Summer humidity in both Moscow and St. Petersburg is moderate. Daytime temperatures average in the 70s, and nights drop to the 50s. By October, the highs average in the 40s and are regularly below freezing from November through March.

RUSSIA

M O S C O W — 505 ft.

	JAN	FEB	MAR	APR	MAY	JUN	JUL	AUG	SEP	OCT	NOV	DEC	ANN.
Av. High °F	21	23	32	47	65	73	76	72	61	46	31	23	47
Av. Low °F	9	10	17	31	44	51	55	52	43	34	23	13	32
Humidity	V.Lo	V.Lo	V.Lo	V.Lo	Lo	Med	Med	Med	Lo	V.Lo	V.Lo	V.Lo	V.Lo
Precip. Days	11	9	8	9	9	10	12	12	9	11	10	9	119
Precip. In.	1.5	1.4	1.1	1.9	2.2	2.9	3.0	2.9	1.9	2.7	1.7	1.6	24.8
Snowfall In.	15	14	9	2	0	0	0	0	0	4	14	16	74

ST. PETERSBURG — 16 ft.

	JAN	FEB	MAR	APR	MAY	JUN	JUL	AUG	SEP	OCT	NOV	DEC	ANN.
Av. High °F	23	24	33	45	58	66	71	66	57	45	34	26	46
Av. Low °F	12	12	18	31	42	51	57	53	45	37	27	18	33
Humidity	V.Lo	V.Lo	V.Lo	V.Lo	Lo	Lo	Med	Med	Lo	V.Lo	V.Lo	V.Lo	V.Lo
Precip. Days	17	15	13	11	12	12	13	15	14	15	17	18	173
Precip. In.	1.0	.9	.9	1.0	1.6	2.0	2.5	2.8	2.1	1.8	1.4	1.2	19.2
Snowfall In.	10	9	7	<1	0	0	0	0	0	4	9	12	51

HIGHEST GLOBAL SEA LEVEL PRESSURE: 32.01"
Agata, Siberia U.S.S.R. — December 31, 1968

LOWEST NORTHERN HEMISPHERE TEMPERATURE: -90°F
Verkhoyansk, U.S.S.R. — February 7, 1892

SCANDINAVIA

Most of Scandinavia lies above the 55 degree latitude line, placing it roughly as far north as Alaska. However, its climate is mild thanks to the warming influence of the Gulf Stream. This warm river of water flows north from the east coast of Florida, then crosses the Atlantic and heads for the Norwegian and Irish coastlines. The Scandinavian climate would be much colder without its influence.

Generous rainfall bathes the mountainous west coast of Norway. These peaks squeeze so much water out of the clouds that roll in off the Atlantic that the fertile lands to the east are relatively dry and often sunnier than one might expect.

The best time to visit Scandinavia is in the late spring and early summer. The longest days occur in late June. Because of the latitude, summer nights are short and barely dark. Rainfall begins to increase in August, and from September through April the weather is uniformly chilly with frequent showers. Snow is common from November through March.

DENMARK

COPENHAGEN — 43 ft.

	JAN	FEB	MAR	APR	MAY	JUN	JUL	AUG	SEP	OCT	NOV	DEC	ANN.
Av. High °F	36	36	41	50	61	67	72	69	63	53	43	38	52
Av. Low °F	29	28	31	37	44	51	55	54	49	42	35	32	41
Humidity	V.Lo	V.Lo	V.Lo	V.Lo	Lo	Med	Med	Med	Med	Lo	V.Lo	V.Lo	Lo
Precip. Days	9	7	8	9	8	8	9	12	8	9	10	11	108
Precip. In.	1.6	1.3	1.2	1.7	1.7	2.1	2.2	3.2	1.9	2.1	2.2	2.1	23.3
Snowfall In.	6	5	3	1	0	0	0	0	0	1	4	5	25

FINLAND

HELSINKI — 30 ft.

	JAN	FEB	MAR	APR	MAY	JUN	JUL	AUG	SEP	OCT	NOV	DEC	ANN.
Av. High °F	27	26	32	43	55	63	71	66	57	45	37	31	46
Av. Low °F	17	15	22	31	41	49	57	55	46	37	30	22	35
Humidity	V.Lo	V.Lo	V.Lo	V.Lo	V.Lo	Lo	Med	Med	Lo	V.Lo	V.Lo	V.Lo	V.Lo
Precip. Days	11	8	8	8	8	9	8	12	11	12	11	11	117
Precip. In.	2.2	1.7	1.7	1.7	1.9	2.0	2.3	3.3	2.8	2.9	2.7	2.4	27.6
Snowfall In.	22	17	12	3	<1	0	0	0	0	6	10	19	89

NORWAY

BERGEN — 141 ft.

	JAN	FEB	MAR	APR	MAY	JUN	JUL	AUG	SEP	OCT	NOV	DEC	ANN.
Av. High °F	43	44	47	55	64	70	72	70	64	57	49	45	57
Av. Low °F	27	26	28	34	41	46	51	50	45	38	33	28	37
Humidity	V.Lo	V.Lo	V.Lo	V.Lo	Lo	Lo	Med	Med	Med	Lo	Lo	V.Lo	Lo
Precip. Days	18	14	13	13	11	13	13	16	17	18	16	18	180
Precip. In.	7.9	6.0	5.4	4.4	3.9	4.2	5.2	7.3	9.2	9.2	8.0	8.1	78.8
Snowfall In.	12	12	6	1	0	0	0	0	0	1	6	8	46

OSLO — 308 ft.

	JAN	FEB	MAR	APR	MAY	JUN	JUL	AUG	SEP	OCT	NOV	DEC	ANN.
Av. High °F	30	32	40	50	62	69	73	69	60	49	37	31	50
Av. Low °F	20	20	25	34	43	51	56	53	45	37	29	24	36
Humidity	V.Lo	V.Lo	V.Lo	V.Lo	V.Lo	Lo	Med	Med	Lo	V.Lo	V.Lo	V.Lo	V.Lo
Precip. Days	8	7	7	7	7	8	10	11	8	10	9	10	102
Precip. In.	1.7	1.3	1.4	1.6	1.8	2.4	2.9	3.8	2.5	2.9	2.3	2.3	26.9
Snowfall In.	13	9	4	1	0	0	0	0	0	2	9	17	55

SWEDEN

STOCKHOLM — 146 ft.

	JAN	FEB	MAR	APR	MAY	JUN	JUL	AUG	SEP	OCT	NOV	DEC	ANN.
Av. High °F	31	31	37	45	57	65	70	66	58	48	38	33	48
Av. Low °F	23	22	26	32	41	49	55	53	46	39	31	26	37
Humidity	V.Lo	V.Lo	V.Lo	V.Lo	V.Lo	Lo	Med	Med	Lo	V.Lo	V.Lo	V.Lo	V.Lo
Precip. Days	8	7	7	6	8	7	9	10	8	9	9	9	97
Precip. In.	1.5	1.1	1.1	1.5	1.6	1.9	2.8	3.1	2.1	2.1	1.9	1.9	22.4
Snowfall In.	10	8	4	2	0	0	0	0	0	3	6	10	43

SPAIN AND PORTUGAL

Lisbon's climate is similar to that of many coastal valleys of Central California. Summers are warm and dry, and winters are cool and wet. The best months to visit are June through August when temperatures are in the 70s during the day, and in the 60s at night, and rain falls only once or twice a month.

Spain is a bit drier—its mountains block the storms sweeping down from the north and west. Summers are very warm, and the humidity is tolerable. Daytime temperatures are in the 80s in most cities, nights average 50s or 60s, and rainfall is infrequent. The best months to visit are May through September. The driest month is August.

SPAIN

BARCELONA — 312 ft.

	JAN	FEB	MAR	APR	MAY	JUN	JUL	AUG	SEP	OCT	NOV	DEC	ANN.
Av. High °F	56	57	61	64	71	77	81	82	78	71	62	57	68
Av. Low °F	42	44	47	51	57	63	69	69	65	58	50	44	55
Humidity	V.Lo	V.Lo	Lo	Lo	Med	Med	Hi	Hi	Med	Med	Lo	V.Lo	Lo
Precip. Days	5	7	7	8	8	5	4	5	7	8	7	6	77
Precip. In.	1.2	2.1	1.9	1.8	1.8	1.3	1.2	1.7	2.6	3.4	2.7	1.8	23.5
Snowfall In.	<1	0	0	0	0	0	0	0	0	0	0	<1	<1

M A D R I D — 2,188 ft.

	JAN	FEB	MAR	APR	MAY	JUN	JUL	AUG	SEP	OCT	NOV	DEC	ANN.
Av. High °F	47	51	57	64	71	80	87	86	77	66	54	48	66
Av. Low °F	33	35	40	44	50	57	62	62	56	48	40	35	47
Humidity	V.Lo	V.Lo	V.Lo	Lo	Lo	Med	Med	Med	Med	Lo	Lo	V.Lo	Lo
Precip. Days	9	9	11	9	9	6	3	2	6	8	10	9	91
Precip. In.	1.1	1.7	1.7	1.7	1.5	1.2	.4	.3	1.2	1.9	2.2	1.6	16.5
Snowfall In.	1	<1	0	0	0	0	0	0	0	0	0	<1	2

PORTUGAL

L I S B O N — 313 ft.

	JAN	FEB	MAR	APR	MAY	JUN	JUL	AUG	SEP	OCT	NOV	DEC	ANN.
Av. High °F	56	58	61	64	69	75	79	80	76	69	62	57	67
Av. Low °F	46	47	49	52	56	60	63	64	62	57	52	47	55
Humidity	Lo	Lo	Lo	Lo	Med	Med	Med	Med	Med	Med	Lo	Lo	Lo
Precip. Days	9	8	10	7	6	2	1	6	4	7	10	10	75
Precip. In.	3.3	3.2	3.1	2.4	1.7	.7	.2	.2	1.4	3.1	4.2	3.6	27.0
Snowfall In.	0	0	0	0	0	0	0	0	0	0	0	0	0

HIGHEST EUROPEAN TEMPERATURE: 122°F
Seville, Spain — August 4, 1881

CHAPTER 5

Africa

The continent of Africa offers a wide variety of climates, ranging from extremely wet and tropical to extremely dry and barren. Along the coast of South Africa, the climate can be as pleasant as any in the world. In the African interior, the climate can be as hostile as any on the planet.

Along the Mediterranean, temperatures are mild and rainfall infrequent. Casablanca, Morocco boasts a superb climate marred only by high humidity in the summer. The best months to visit are May and October.

It's best to visit Egypt and the pyramids in the spring or fall—especially April and November. Summers are hot, humid, and dry. Even in the winter, rainfall is scant, but temperatures resemble Los Angeles in January. All months except June through September are tolerably mild.

A visit to Kenya and Mount Kilimanjaro will take you to the city of Nairobi at 5,971 ft. elevation. Temperatures here are uniformly comfortable all year long, with highs ranging from 69 to 79 during the afternoon, and nighttime temperatures in the 50s. Rainfall increases during March through May, with heavy amounts expected several times a week.

The best time to visit is during the dry months of June through September (particularly September).

South Africa is a land of mountains and beaches, with spectacular scenery and a climate to match. Johannesburg can get quite cool in the Southern Hemisphere's winter season of May through September. Temperatures are mild during the summer, but rains are common at that time.

The best months to visit are in the spring and fall if you want daytime temperatures in the 70's and rainfall that isn't too frequent. At lower elevations the weather can seem much like the Southern California beach cities, with mild temperatures, low rainfall, and miles of beaches and surf for scenery. Any month from November through March would be enjoyable.

EGYPT

C A I R O — 381 ft.

	JAN	FEB	MAR	APR	MAY	JUN	JUL	AUG	SEP	OCT	NOV	DEC	ANN.
Av. High °F	65	69	75	83	91	95	96	95	90	86	78	68	83
Av. Low °F	47	48	52	57	63	68	70	71	68	65	58	50	60
Humidity	Lo	V.Lo	Lo	Lo	Med	Med	Hi	Hi	Hi	Med	Med	Lo	Med
Precip. Days	1	1	1	<1	<1	0	0	0	0	<1	1	1	5
Precip. In.	.2	.2	.2	.1	.1	0	0	0	0	0	.1	.2	1.1
Snowfall In.	0	0	0	0	0	0	0	0	0	0	0	0	0

KENYA

N A I R O B I — 5,971 ft.

	JAN	FEB	MAR	APR	MAY	JUN	JUL	AUG	SEP	OCT	NOV	DEC	ANN.
Av. High °F	77	79	77	75	72	70	69	70	75	76	74	74	74
Av. Low °F	54	55	57	58	56	53	51	52	52	55	56	55	55
Humidity	Med	Med	Med	Hi	Med	Med	Med	Med	Med	Med	Med	Med	Med
Precip. Days	5	6	11	16	17	9	6	7	6	8	15	11	117
Precip. In.	1.5	2.5	4.9	8.3	6.2	1.8	.6	.9	1.2	2.1	4.3	3.4	37.7
Snowfall In.	0	0	0	0	0	0	0	0	0	0	0	0	0

MOROCCO

C A S A B L A N C A — 164 ft.

	JAN	FEB	MAR	APR	MAY	JUN	JUL	AUG	SEP	OCT	NOV	DEC	ANN.
Av. High °F	63	64	67	69	72	76	79	81	79	76	69	65	72
Av. Low °F	45	46	49	52	56	61	65	66	63	58	52	47	55
Humidity	Lo	Lo	Med	Med	Med	Hi	Hi	Hi	Hi	Med	Med	Med	Med
Precip. Days	8	8	8	7	5	1	0	0	1	6	8	9	61
Precip. In.	2.1	1.9	2.2	1.4	.9	.2	0	0	.3	1.5	2.6	2.8	15.9
Snowfall In.	0	0	0	0	0	0	0	0	0	0	0	0	0

SOUTH AFRICA

C A P E   T O W N — 56 ft.

	JAN	FEB	MAR	APR	MAY	JUN	JUL	AUG	SEP	OCT	NOV	DEC	ANN.
Av. High °F	69	70	69	66	64	62	60	61	63	65	67	69	65
Av. Low °F	56	56	56	54	53	51	50	50	50	53	54	55	53
Humidity	Med	Med	Med	Med	Med	Med	Lo	Med	Lo	Med	Med	Med	Med
Precip. Days	3	2	3	6	9	9	10	9	7	5	3	3	69
Precip. In.	.1	.1	.3	.9	1.3	1.7	1.6	1.0	1.0	.5	.2	.3	9.0
Snowfall In.	0	0	0	0	0	0	0	0	0	0	0	0	0

J O H A N N E S B U R G — 5,463 ft.

	JAN	FEB	MAR	APR	MAY	JUN	JUL	AUG	SEP	OCT	NOV	DEC	ANN.
Av. High °F	78	77	75	72	66	62	63	68	73	77	77	78	72
Av. Low °F	58	58	55	50	43	39	39	43	48	53	55	57	50
Humidity	Med	Med	Med	Med	Lo	Lo	Lo	Lo	Lo	Med	Med	Med	Med
Precip. Days	12	9	9	4	3	1	.9	.9	2	7	10	11	70
Precip. In.	4.5	4.3	3.5	1.5	1.0	.3	.3	.3	.9	2.2	4.2	4.9	27.9
Snowfall In.	0	0	0	0	0	0	0	0	0	0	0	0	0

LOWEST GLOBAL PRECIPITATION IN ONE YEAR: 0.00"
Kharga, Egypt (Dec. '57-Mar. '60), Wadi Halfa,
Sudan (Jun. '45-Apr. '49)

CHAPTER 6

Middle East

ISRAEL

The climate of Israel is marked by distinct seasons. Summers are warm, humid, and dry. Winters are cool, with low humidity, but rainfall is plentiful. The spring months are the most pleasant. In particular, the month of April offers the best combination of mild temperatures, moderate humidity, and few rainy days. Jerusalem has lower humidity than coastal areas because of its elevation: 2,485 feet. Towns bordering the Mediterranean can be quite humid during the summer.

ISRAEL

JERUSALEM — 2,485 ft.

	JAN	FEB	MAR	APR	MAY	JUN	JUL	AUG	SEP	OCT	NOV	DEC	ANN.
Av. High °F	55	56	65	73	81	85	87	87	85	81	70	59	73
Av. Low °F	41	42	46	50	57	60	63	64	62	59	53	45	53
Humidity	V.Lo	V.Lo	V.Lo	V.Lo	Lo	Lo	Med	Med	Med	Lo	Lo	V.Lo	Lo
Precip. Days	9	11	3	3	1	0	0	0	0	1	4	7	39
Precip. In.	5.2	5.2	2.5	1.1	.1	0	0	0	0	.5	2.8	3.4	20.8
Snowfall In.	0	0	0	0	0	0	0	0	0	0	0	0	0

TEL AVIV — 33 ft.

	JAN	FEB	MAR	APR	MAY	JUN	JUL	AUG	SEP	OCT	NOV	DEC	ANN.
Av. High °F	64	64	66	70	74	79	82	83	82	79	73	67	74
Av. Low °F	50	51	53	57	62	68	72	74	71	65	58	53	61
Humidity	Lo	Lo	Med	Med	Hi	Hi	V.Hi	V.Hi	Hi	Hi	Med	Lo	Med
Precip. Days	9	5	5	2	2	0	0	2	1	1	6	12	45
Precip. In.	4.6	2.4	2.0	1.0	1.4	0	0	1.7	.2	.5	4.8	12.9	31.5
Snowfall In.	0	0	0	0	0	0	0	0	0	0	0	0	0

TURKEY

The primary business and tourist center of Turkey is the historic city of Istanbul. Summers are warm and humid with occasional rainfall. Winters are chilly with frequent rainy days. The best times to visit are late spring and early fall. In particular, May offers the best mix of the elements, although it does rain an average of five days during that month.

TURKEY

ISTANBUL — 59 ft.

	JAN	FEB	MAR	APR	MAY	JUN	JUL	AUG	SEP	OCT	NOV	DEC	ANN.
Av. High °F	45	47	52	61	68	77	81	81	75	67	59	51	64
Av. Low °F	36	37	39	45	53	60	65	66	61	54	48	41	50
Humidity	V.Lo	V.Lo	Lo	Lo	Med	Hi	Hi	Hi	Hi	Med	Lo	Lo	Med
Precip. Days	12	10	9	6	5	4	3	3	5	9	11	15	92
Precip. In.	3.7	2.3	2.6	1.9	1.4	1.3	1.7	1.5	2.3	3.8	4.1	4.9	31.5
Snowfall In.	8	6	0	0	0	0	0	0	0	0	0	2	16

SAUDI ARABIAN PENINSULA

The oil-producing lands of Kuwait and Saudi Arabia are known for their hot and dry summers with afternoon temperatures averaging above 100 degrees. However, winter temperatures are pleasant. The best months to visit are late fall and early spring. November and March offer a nice combination of mild temperatures, low humidity, and sunny skies, with few rainy days. Months to avoid are May through October, and in particular July and August—unless you like it hot, with nights staying in the 70s and 80s!

KUWAIT

KUWAIT CITY — 16 ft.

	JAN	FEB	MAR	APR	MAY	JUN	JUL	AUG	SEP	OCT	NOV	DEC	ANN.
Av. High °F	61	65	72	83	94	98	103	104	100	91	77	65	85
Av. Low °F	49	51	59	68	77	82	86	86	81	73	62	53	69
Humidity	Lo	Lo	Lo	Med	Med	Lo	Med	Med	Med	Med	Med	Lo	Lo
Precip. Days	3	3	3	1	0	0	0	0	0	1	2	3	16
Precip. In.	.9	.9	1.1	.2	0	0	0	0	0	.1	.6	1.1	5.1
Snowfall In.	0	0	0	0	0	0	0	0	0	0	0	0	0

SAUDI ARABIA

RIYADH — 1,938 ft.

	JAN	FEB	MAR	APR	MAY	JUN	JUL	AUG	SEP	OCT	NOV	DEC	ANN.
Av. High °F	70	73	82	89	100	107	107	107	102	94	84	70	90
Av. Low °F	46	48	56	64	72	77	78	75	72	61	55	49	63
Humidity	V.Lo	V.Lo	V.Lo	Lo	Lo	V.Lo	V.Lo	V.Lo	V.Lo	V.Lo	Lo	V.Lo	V.Lo
Precip. Days	1	1	3	4	1	0	0	0	0	0	0	0	10
Precip. In.	.1	.8	.9	1.0	.4	0	0	0	0	0	0	0	3.2
Snowfall In.	0	0	0	0	0	0	0	0	0	0	0	0	0

HIGHEST ASIAN TEMPERATURE: 129°F
Tirat Tsvi, Israel — June 21, 1942

HIGHEST GLOBAL TEMPERATURE: 136°F
El Azizia, Libya — September 13, 1922

Part III

Asia
Australia
New Zealand
South Pacific

CHAPTER 7

Asia

CHINA, JAPAN, SOUTH KOREA, AND TAIWAN

China is uniformly warm, humid, and rainy in the summer. In contrast, winter weather can vary considerably from city to city. Beijing, for example, is very cold in the winter, with afternoon highs averaging only 34 degrees. Shanghai's January high is only 46. Hong Kong's tropical climate keeps it mild even in January, when highs are in the 60s. Rainfall in China is concentrated primarily in the summer months—July in particular should be avoided due to its high heat, humidity, and generous rainfall.

The best times to visit Beijing are in the early fall and late spring, especially May and September, with April and October almost as pleasant. Humidity, however, can be high from June through September. Shanghai is very pleasant in October and May. Taiwan is driest in the winter. Humidity there is high from April through October. Hong Kong's best months are November through April. Humidity there is very high from May through September. Rainfall can be torrential in June through

August and the island is visited by occasional typhoons (hurricanes) at that time.

Japan is also very warm, humid, and wet in the summer. Winters can be chilly. The best month to visit Tokyo is May. Rainfall there peaks in September and October. Osaka is a bit warmer than Tokyo and can also be extremely humid and wet during the summer. May and October are the best months to visit.

South Korea's climate can be extreme: very cold in the winter and tropical in the summer. Rain is most common in July and August. The most enjoyable months to visit are May and late September through early October.

CHINA

BEIJING — 167 ft.

	JAN	FEB	MAR	APR	MAY	JUN	JUL	AUG	SEP	OCT	NOV	DEC	ANN.
Av. High °F	34	43	54	69	81	88	89	86	79	66	50	39	65
Av. Low °F	15	21	32	44	56	65	72	69	58	44	31	20	44
Humidity	V.Lo	V.Lo	Lo	Med	Med	Hi	V.Hi	V.Hi	Hi	Med	Lo	V.Lo	Med
Precip. Days	2	2	2	3	5	8	15	11	8	2	1	2	61
Precip. In.	.2	.2	.3	.6	1.3	3.3	9.8	5.7	2.3	.7	.2	.1	24.7
Snowfall In.	7	4	1	0	0	0	0	0	0	0	1	3	16

SHANGHAI — 23 ft.

	JAN	FEB	MAR	APR	MAY	JUN	JUL	AUG	SEP	OCT	NOV	DEC	ANN.
Av. High °F	46	47	55	66	77	82	90	90	82	74	63	53	69
Av. Low °F	33	34	40	50	59	67	74	74	66	57	45	36	53
Humidity	V.Lo	V.Lo	Lo	Med	Med	Hi	V.Hi	V.Hi	Hi	Med	Lo	V.Lo	Med
Precip. Days	6	9	9	9	9	11	9	9	11	4	6	6	98
Precip. In.	1.9	2.3	3.3	3.7	3.7	7.1	5.8	5.6	5.1	2.8	2.0	1.4	44.7
Snowfall In.	0	0	0	0	0	0	0	0	0	0	0	0	0

HONG KONG

HONG KONG — 109 ft.

	JAN	FEB	MAR	APR	MAY	JUN	JUL	AUG	SEP	OCT	NOV	DEC	ANN.
Av. High °F	64	63	67	75	82	85	87	87	85	81	74	68	77
Av. Low °F	56	55	60	67	74	78	78	78	77	73	65	59	68
Humidity	Med	Med	Med	Hi	V.Hi	V.Hi	V.Hi	V.Hi	V.Hi	Hi	Hi	Med	Hi
Precip. Days	4	5	7	8	13	18	17	15	12	6	2	3	110
Precip. In.	1.3	1.8	2.9	5.4	11.5	15.5	15.0	14.2	10.1	4.5	1.7	1.2	85.1
Snowfall In.	0	0	0	0	0	0	0	0	0	0	0	0	0

JAPAN

O S A K A — 10 ft.

	JAN	FEB	MAR	APR	MAY	JUN	JUL	AUG	SEP	OCT	NOV	DEC	ANN.
Av. High °F	47	48	54	65	73	80	87	90	83	72	62	52	68
Av. Low °F	32	33	37	47	55	64	73	74	67	55	44	37	51
Humidity	V.Lo	V.Lo	V.Lo	Lo	Med	Hi	V.Hi	V.Hi	Hi	Med	Lo	V.Lo	Med
Precip. Days	6	6	9	10	10	11	9	7	11	9	7	6	101
Precip. In.	1.7	2.3	3.8	5.2	4.9	7.4	5.9	4.4	7.0	5.1	3.0	1.9	52.6
Snowfall In.	1	1	0	0	0	0	0	0	0	0	0	0	2

T O K Y O — 19 ft.

	JAN	FEB	MAR	APR	MAY	JUN	JUL	AUG	SEP	OCT	NOV	DEC	ANN.
Av. High °F	47	48	54	63	71	76	83	86	79	69	60	52	66
Av. Low °F	29	31	36	46	54	63	70	72	66	55	43	33	50
Humidity	V.Lo	V.Lo	V.Lo	Lo	Med	Hi	V.Hi	V.Hi	Hi	Med	Lo	V.Lo	Med
Precip. Days	5	6	10	10	10	12	10	9	12	11	7	5	107
Precip. In.	1.9	2.9	4.2	5.3	5.8	6.5	5.6	6.0	9.2	8.2	3.8	2.2	61.6
Snowfall In.	2	5	1	0	0	0	0	0	0	0	0	0	8

SOUTH KOREA

S E O U L — 285 ft.

	JAN	FEB	MAR	APR	MAY	JUN	JUL	AUG	SEP	OCT	NOV	DEC	ANN.
Av. High °F	32	37	47	62	72	80	84	87	78	67	51	37	61
Av. Low °F	15	20	29	41	51	61	70	71	59	45	32	20	43
Humidity	V.Lo	V.Lo	V.Lo	Lo	Med	Hi	V.Hi	V.Hi	Hi	Lo	V.Lo	V.Lo	Lo
Precip. Days	8	6	7	8	10	10	16	13	9	7	9	9	112
Precip. In.	1.2	.8	1.5	3.0	3.2	51	14.8	10.5	4.7	1.6	1.8	1.0	49.2
Snowfall In.	5	4	1	0	0	0	0	0	0	0	0	1	11

TAIWAN

T A I P E I — 30 ft.

	JAN	FEB	MAR	APR	MAY	JUN	JUL	AUG	SEP	OCT	NOV	DEC	ANN.
Av. High °F	66	65	70	77	83	89	92	91	88	81	75	69	79
Av. Low °F	54	53	57	63	69	73	76	75	73	67	62	57	65
Humidity	Med	Med	Med	Hi	V.Hi	V.Hi	V.Hi	V.Hi	V.Hi	Hi	Hi	Med	Hi
Precip. Days	9	13	12	14	12	13	10	12	10	9	7	8	129
Precip. In.	3.4	5.3	7.0	6.7	9.1	11.4	9.1	12.0	9.6	4.8	2.6	2.8	83.8
Snowfall In.	0	0	0	0	0	0	0	0	0	0	0	0	0

THE PHILIPPINES AND
SOUTHEAST ASIA

The Philippines, and all of Southeast Asia, are tropical, and hence uniformly warm, humid, and rainy. While there is a dry season in the Philippines and Thailand, Singapore is rainy all year long. The best time to visit Manila is in January and February, when rainfall is light and temperatures are moderately warm. Months to be avoided are June through September. Bangkok and much of Southeast Asia have a dry season during the winter months. The best months to visit are December through February. Bangkok is wettest in September, although it's also very rainy from May through August.

One of the most popular travel destinations in the world is Bali, a beautiful, lush island in Indonesia. You will not need a jacket in Bali. Temperatures are consistently warm and humidity is high throughout the year. Bali experiences a distinct rainy season, peaking in December and January when rainfall can be heavy and frequent. The driest months are May through September. The best months to visit are August and September, when rainfall is low. Jakarta, Indonesia has a climate similar to Bali—that is, it is consistently warm and tropical with most rainfall from December through March. The best time to visit would be during the relatively coolest and driest months of July, August, and September.

Kuala Lumpur, Malaysia is consistently warm, tropical, humid, and rainy. It is also lush and beautiful. High temperatures vary little through the year, and average 88 to 91 degrees during the day, and 73 to 74 at night. Rainfall varies from 5 inches per month in February and June to over 10 inches on the average from October to December. The pattern of temperature and rainfall is so even throughout the year that there is no best month to visit, although the weather records show February to be the driest month.

Vietnam is becoming a popular travel and business destination. Temperatures are consistently warm in Saigon/Ho Chi Minh City. Highs average 87 to 94 through the year, with lows in the 70s. Humidity is always high. There is a distinct rainy season from May through October. The driest months are January, February, and March, with almost no rainfall during February.

INDONESIA

B A L I — 16 ft.

	JAN	FEB	MAR	APR	MAY	JUN	JUL	AUG	SEP	OCT	NOV	DEC	ANN.
Av. High °F	90	89	90	91	90	88	87	86	88	89	91	90	89
Av. Low °F	73	73	73	72	72	70	68	71	71	71	72	71	71
Humidity	V.Hi	V.Hi	V.Hi	V.Hi	V.Hi	Hi	Hi	Hi	Hi	Hi	V.Hi	V.Hi	V.Hi
Precip. Days	19	19	16	12	10	8	6	3	5	6	14	21	139
Precip. In.	15.9	8.4	8.1	5.0	1.6	2.0	3.4	1.5	.4	4.8	7.9	14.7	74.3

J A K A R T A — 98 ft.

	JAN	FEB	MAR	APR	MAY	JUN	JUL	AUG	SEP	OCT	NOV	DEC	ANN.
Av. High °F	83	85	86	88	88	88	88	88	89	89	88	86	87
Av. Low °F	75	75	75	76	76	75	74	74	75	76	76	75	75
Humidity	V.Hi	V.Hi	V.Hi	V.Hi	V.Hi	V.Hi	V.Hi	V.Hi	V.Hi	V.Hi	V.Hi	V.Hi	V.Hi
Precip. Days	19	14	14	11	8	5	5	5	5	8	11	14	119
Precip. In.	11.8	11.8	8.3	5.8	5.2	3.8	2.5	1.7	2.6	4.4	5.6	8.0	71.5

MALAYSIA

K U A L A L U M P U R — 89 ft.

	JAN	FEB	MAR	APR	MAY	JUN	JUL	AUG	SEP	OCT	NOV	DEC	ANN.
Av. High °F	89	90	91	90	90	90	89	89	89	89	88	88	89
Av. Low °F	73	73	74	75	75	74	74	74	74	74	74	73	74
Humidity	V.Hi	V.Hi	V.Hi	V.Hi	V.Hi	V.Hi	V.Hi	V.Hi	V.Hi	V.Hi	V.Hi	V.Hi	V.Hi
Precip. Days	16	16	19	21	19	14	15	15	20	22	25	22	224
Precip. In.	6.8	4.8	10.4	11.5	9.0	5.4	6.0	7.3	8.2	11.2	13.9	11.3	105.7

PHILIPPINES

M A N I L A — 47 ft.

	JAN	FEB	MAR	APR	MAY	JUN	JUL	AUG	SEP	OCT	NOV	DEC	ANN.
Av. High °F	86	88	91	93	93	91	88	87	88	88	87	86	89
Av. Low °F	69	69	71	73	75	75	75	75	75	74	72	70	73
Humidity	Hi	Hi	Hi	V.Hi	V.Hi	V.Hi	V.Hi	V.Hi	V.Hi	V.Hi	V.Hi	V.Hi	V.Hi
Precip. Days	6	3	4	4	12	17	24	23	22	19	14	11	159
Precip. In.	.9	.5	.7	1.3	5.1	10.0	17.0	16.6	14.0	7.6	5.7	2.6	82.0

SINGAPORE

S I N G A P O R E — 33 ft.

	JAN	FEB	MAR	APR	MAY	JUN	JUL	AUG	SEP	OCT	NOV	DEC	ANN.
Av. High °F	86	88	88	88	89	88	88	87	87	87	87	87	87
Av. Low °F	73	73	75	75	75	75	75	75	75	74	74	74	74
Humidity	V.Hi	V.Hi	V.Hi	V.Hi	V.Hi	V.Hi	V.Hi	V.Hi	V.Hi	V.Hi	V.Hi	V.Hi	V.Hi
Precip. Days	17	11	14	15	15	13	13	14	14	16	18	19	179
Precip. In.	9.9	6.8	7.6	7.4	6.8	6.8	6.7	7.7	7.0	8.2	10.0	10.1	95.0

THAILAND

B A N G K O K — 7 ft.

	JAN	FEB	MAR	APR	MAY	JUN	JUL	AUG	SEP	OCT	NOV	DEC	ANN.
Av. High °F	89	91	93	95	93	91	90	90	89	88	87	87	90
Av. Low °F	68	72	75	77	77	76	76	76	76	75	72	68	74
Humidity	Hi	V.Hi	V.Hi	V.Hi	V.Hi	V.Hi	V.Hi	V.Hi	V.Hi	V.Hi	V.Hi	Hi	V.Hi
Precip. Days	1	1	3	3	9	10	13	13	15	14	5	1	88
Precip. In.	.3	.8	1.4	2.3	7.8	6.3	6.3	6.9	12.0	8.1	2.6	.2	55.0

VIETNAM

S A I G O N — 33 ft.

	JAN	FEB	MAR	APR	MAY	JUN	JUL	AUG	SEP	OCT	NOV	DEC	ANN.
Av. High °F	89	91	93	94	92	89	88	89	88	88	87	87	90
Av. Low °F	70	71	74	77	76	75	75	75	75	74	73	71	74
Humidity	Hi	Hi	V.Hi	V.Hi	V.Hi	V.Hi	V.Hi	V.Hi	V.Hi	V.Hi	V.Hi	V.Hi	V.Hi
Precip. Days	1	1	1	4	5	16	16	15	15	13	8	4	98
Precip. In.	.6	.2	.4	2.0	8.6	12.4	11.7	10.7	13.0	10.2	4.6	2.1	76.5

INDIA

Many people think of India as always hot and humid. However, some months can be very pleasant, with winter being the best time to visit. February is generally ideal all around for moderate temperature, humidity, and low rainfall. Summers are to be avoided. Not only are they hot, but the humidity is high and rainfall heavy. In Bombay, January and February temperatures reach 83 and it only rains once a month on the average.

New Delhi's climate can be extreme. In May, just before the monsoon rains arrive, highs average 105. In January, highs average 70 degrees with chilly nights dropping to 44. The general rule is that the farther north you travel, the cooler it gets, although most of the country lies either in the tropics or subtropics and is surrounded by the warm waters of the Bay of Bengal and the Arabian Sea.

INDIA

B O M B A Y — 37 ft.

	JAN	FEB	MAR	APR	MAY	JUN	JUL	AUG	SEP	OCT	NOV	DEC	ANN.
Av. High °F	83	83	86	89	91	89	85	85	85	89	89	87	87
Av. Low °F	67	67	72	76	80	79	77	76	76	76	73	69	74
Humidity	Med	Med	Hi	V.Hi	V.Hi	V.Hi	V.Hi	V.Hi	V.Hi	V.Hi	Hi	Med	Hi
Precip. Days	1	1	1	0	2	18	23	21	15	5	3	1	91
Precip. In.	.1	.1	.1	0	.7	19.1	24.3	13.4	10.4	2.5	.5	.1	71.2

C A L C U T T A — 21 ft.

	JAN	FEB	MAR	APR	MAY	JUN	JUL	AUG	SEP	OCT	NOV	DEC	ANN.
Av. High °F	80	84	93	97	96	92	89	89	90	89	84	79	89
Av. Low °F	55	59	69	75	77	79	79	78	78	74	64	55	70
Humidity	Med	Med	Hi	V.Hi	V.Hi	V.Hi	V.Hi	V.Hi	V.Hi	V.Hi	Hi	Med	Hi
Precip. Days	3	5	5	6	10	16	18	18	13	6	3	2	105
Precip. In.	.4	1.2	1.4	1.7	5.5	11.7	12.8	12.9	9.9	4.5	.8	.2	63.0

N E W   D E L H I — 714 ft.

	JAN	FEB	MAR	APR	MAY	JUN	JUL	AUG	SEP	OCT	NOV	DEC	ANN.
Av. High °F	70	75	87	97	105	102	96	93	93	93	84	73	89
Av. Low °F	44	49	58	68	79	83	81	79	75	65	52	46	65
Humidity	Lo	Lo	Lo	Med	Med	Hi	V.Hi	V.Hi	V.Hi	Hi	Lo	Lo	Med
Precip. Days	2	2	1	1	2	4	8	8	4	1	.2	1	34
Precip. In.	.9	.7	.5	.3	.5	2.9	7.1	6.8	4.6	.4	.1	.4	25.2

GREATEST GLOBAL PRECIPITATION IN 1 MONTH: 366.14"
Cherrapunji, India — July 1861

GREATEST GLOBAL PRECIPITATION IN 1 YEAR: 1,041.78"
Cherrapunji, India — August 1860 to July 1861

CHAPTER 8

Australia, New Zealand, and the South Pacific

AUSTRALIA

Three primary climates dominate the continent of Australia. The north is tropical, warm, humid, and rainy. Most of the interior is hot, barren, and rather desolate. The coastal strip is generally warm and somewhat humid. Rainfall varies from generous in Queensland to sparse in Victoria. This narrow, flat, scenic plain is home to most Australians and boasts some of the most beautiful and pleasant weather on earth.

For year-round mild to warm temperatures, few areas can top coastal Queensland near Brisbane, called the Gold Coast. In general, the weather is a match for Hawaii or other semi-tropical resort areas. The best months to visit are May and September through October, before the humidity and rainfall increase.

The greater Sydney area boasts a magnificent, mild temperature pattern. Rainfall, cloudiness, and humidity can be a problem at times. The best combination of moderate temperature and humidity with the least rainfall would be found during October through December.

The climate of Melbourne is much like that of coastal California. It does get chilly here during the Southern Hemisphere's winter months of June through August. Best months to visit are November through March (especially February).

If you want to visit the interior, you'll find Alice Springs a good base. It's hot in the summer, cool in the winter, and averages less than 10 inches of rain per year.

Perth, in Western Australia, boasts a warm climate with moderate rainfall. The driest months are August and September.

AUSTRALIA

ADELAIDE — 13 ft.

	JAN	FEB	MAR	APR	MAY	JUN	JUL	AUG	SEP	OCT	NOV	DEC	ANN.
Av. High °F	86	86	81	73	66	61	59	62	66	73	79	83	73
Av. Low °F	61	62	59	55	50	47	45	46	48	51	55	59	53
Humidity	Lo	Med	Med	Lo	Lo	Lo	Lo	Lo	Lo	Lo	Lo	Lo	Lo
Precip. Days	5	4	6	8	12	12	15	15	12	11	7	7	114
Precip. In.	.8	.7	1.0	1.8	2.7	3.0	2.6	2.6	2.1	1.7	1.1	1.0	21.1
Snowfall In.	0	0	0	0	0	0	0	0	0	0	0	0	0

ALICE SPRINGS — 1,901 ft.

	JAN	FEB	MAR	APR	MAY	JUN	JUL	AUG	SEP	OCT	NOV	DEC	ANN.
Av. High °F	97	95	90	81	73	67	67	73	81	88	93	96	83
Av. Low °F	70	69	63	54	46	41	39	43	49	58	64	68	55
Humidity	Lo	Lo	Lo	Lo	V.Lo	V.Lo	V.Lo	V.Lo	V.lo	V.Lo	V.Lo	Lo	V.Lo
Precip. Days	4	3	3	2	2	2	1	2	1	3	4	4	31
Precip. In.	1.7	1.3	1.1	.4	.6	.5	.3	.3	.3	.7	1.2	1.5	9.9
Snowfall In.	0	0	0	0	0	0	0	0	0	0	0	0	0

BRISBANE — 137 ft.

	JAN	FEB	MAR	APR	MAY	JUN	JUL	AUG	SEP	OCT	NOV	DEC	ANN.
Av. High °F	85	85	82	79	74	69	68	71	76	80	82	85	78
Av. Low °F	69	68	66	61	56	51	49	50	55	60	64	67	60
Humidity	Hi	Hi	Hi	Hi	Med	Med	Lo	Lo	Med	Med	Hi	Hi	Med
Precip. Days	13	14	15	12	10	8	8	7	8	9	10	12	126
Precip. In.	6.4	6.3	5.7	3.7	2.8	2.6	2.2	1.9	1.9	2.5	3.7	5.0	44.7
Snowfall In.	0	0	0	0	0	0	0	0	0	0	0	0	0

MELBOURNE — 115 ft.

	JAN	FEB	MAR	APR	MAY	JUN	JUL	AUG	SEP	OCT	NOV	DEC	ANN.
Av. High °F	78	78	75	68	62	57	56	59	63	67	71	75	67
Av. Low °F	57	57	55	51	47	44	42	43	46	48	51	54	50
Humidity	Med	Med	Med	Med	Lo	Lo	Lo	Lo	Lo	Lo	Med	Med	Med
Precip. Days	9	8	9	13	14	16	17	17	15	14	13	11	156
Precip. In.	1.9	1.8	2.2	2.3	2.1	2.1	1.9	1.9	2.3	2.6	2.3	2.3	25.7
Snowfall In.	0	0	0	0	0	0	0	0	0	0	0	0	0

PERTH — 197 ft.

	JAN	FEB	MAR	APR	MAY	JUN	JUL	AUG	SEP	OCT	NOV	DEC	ANN.
Av. High °F	85	85	81	76	69	64	63	64	67	70	76	81	73
Av. Low °F	63	63	61	57	53	50	48	48	50	53	57	61	55
Humidity	Med	Med	Med	Med	Med	Med	Lo	Lo	Lo	Med	Med	Med	Med
Precip. Days	3	3	5	8	15	17	19	19	15	12	7	5	128
Precip. In.	.3	.4	.8	1.7	5.1	7.1	6.7	5.7	3.4	2.2	.8	.5	34.7
Snowfall In.	0	0	0	0	0	0	0	0	0	0	0	0	0

SYDNEY — 138 ft.

	JAN	FEB	MAR	APR	MAY	JUN	JUL	AUG	SEP	OCT	NOV	DEC	ANN.
Av. High °F	78	78	76	71	66	61	60	63	67	71	74	77	70
Av. Low °F	65	65	63	58	52	48	46	48	51	56	60	63	56
Humidity	Hi	Hi	Hi	Med	Lo	Lo	Lo	Lo	Lo	Med	Med	Med	Med
Precip. Days	14	13	14	14	13	12	12	11	12	12	12	13	152
Precip. In.	3.5	4.0	5.0	5.3	5.0	4.6	4.6	3.0	2.9	2.8	2.9	2.9	46.5
Snowfall In.	0	0	0	0	0	0	0	0	0	0	0	0	0

HIGHEST AUSTRALIAN TEMPERATURE: 128°F
Cloncurry, Queensland — January 16, 1889

NEW ZEALAND

Most of New Zealand is farther south, and hence cooler, than most of Australia. On the North Island, Auckland enjoys a mild climate with frequent rainfall. The best time to visit would be December through March, although it can get a bit muggy at times.

Wellington is cooler than Auckland. Rainfall here is common, although humidity isn't much of a problem. The best months to visit are January through March. The winter months can be very wet and chilly.

The climate of the South Island is quite cool and showery. In spite of these drawbacks the beauty of the area is legendary. Much of the precipitation falls as snow at higher elevations, creating some of the most spectacular alpine scenery on earth. The climate of Christchurch resembles coastal Washington and Oregon. Temperatures are cool, and rainfall is frequent. The mildest weather occurs from November through March.

NEW ZEALAND

A U C K L A N D — 85 ft.

	JAN	FEB	MAR	APR	MAY	JUN	JUL	AUG	SEP	OCT	NOV	DEC	ANN.
Av. High °F	73	73	71	67	62	58	56	58	60	63	66	70	65
Av. Low °F	60	60	59	56	51	48	46	46	49	52	54	57	53
Humidity	Hi	Hi	Med	Med	Med	Lo	Lo	Lo	Lo	Med	Med	Med	Med
Precip. Days	10	10	11	14	19	19	21	19	17	16	15	12	183
Precip. In.	3.1	3.7	3.2	3.8	5.0	5.4	5.7	4.6	4.0	4.0	3.5	3.1	49.1
Snowfall In.	0	0	0	0	0	0	0	0	0	0	0	0	0

C H R I S T C H U R C H — 32 ft.

	JAN	FEB	MAR	APR	MAY	JUN	JUL	AUG	SEP	OCT	NOV	DEC	ANN.
Av. High °F	70	69	66	62	56	51	50	52	57	62	66	69	61
Av. Low °F	53	53	50	45	40	36	35	36	40	44	47	51	44
Humidity	Lo	Med	Lo	Lo	Lo	Lo	V.Lo	V.Lo	V.Lo	V.Lo	Lo	Lo	Lo
Precip. Days	10	8	9	10	12	13	13	11	10	10	10	10	126
Precip. In.	2.2	1.7	1.9	1.9	2.6	2.6	2.7	1.9	1.8	1.7	1.9	2.2	25.1
Snowfall In.	0	0	0	0	0	0	0	0	0	0	0	0	0

W E L L I N G T O N — 415 ft.

	JAN	FEB	MAR	APR	MAY	JUN	JUL	AUG	SEP	OCT	NOV	DEC	ANN.
Av. High °F	69	69	67	63	58	55	53	54	57	60	63	67	61
Av. Low °F	56	56	54	51	47	44	42	43	46	48	50	54	49
Humidity	Med	Med	Med	Lo	Lo	Lo	Lo	Lo	Lo	Lo	Lo	Med	Lo
Precip. Days	10	9	11	13	16	17	18	17	15	14	13	12	165
Precip. In.	3.2	3.2	3.2	3.8	4.6	4.6	5.4	4.6	3.8	4.0	3.5	3.5	47.4
Snowfall In.	0	0	0	0	0	0	0	0	0	0	0	0	0

HIGHEST ANTARCTIC TEMPERATURE: 58°F
Esparanza — October 20, 1956

SOUTH PACIFIC

Few areas on Earth can match the beauty of the South Pacific. Tahiti and Fiji lie south of the Equator and hence are warmest and most humid from December through February. The driest months are June through November. The best month to visit for moderate temperature, lower humidity, and the lowest rainfall is August.

FIJI

S U V A — 20 ft.

	JAN	FEB	MAR	APR	MAY	JUN	JUL	AUG	SEP	OCT	NOV	DEC	ANN.
Av. High °F	86	86	86	84	82	80	79	79	80	81	83	85	83
Av. Low °F	74	74	74	73	71	69	68	68	69	70	71	73	71
Humidity	V.Hi	V.Hi	V.Hi	V.Hi	V.Hi	Hi	Hi	Hi	Hi	Hi	Hi	V.Hi	Hi
Precip. Days	18	18	21	19	16	13	14	15	16	15	15	18	108
Precip. In.	11.4	10.7	14.5	12.2	10.1	6.7	4.9	8.3	7.7	8.3	9.8	12.5	117.1

TAHITI

P A P E E T E — 302 ft.

	JAN	FEB	MAR	APR	MAY	JUN	JUL	AUG	SEP	OCT	NOV	DEC	ANN.
Av. High °F	89	89	89	89	87	86	86	86	86	87	88	88	88
Av. Low °F	72	72	72	72	70	69	68	68	69	70	71	72	70
Humidity	V.Hi	V.Hi	V.Hi	V.Hi	V.Hi	V.Hi	V.Hi	V.Hi	V.Hi	V.Hi	V.Hi	V.Hi	V.Hi
Precip. Days	16	16	17	10	10	8	5	6	6	9	13	14	130
Precip. In.	9.9	9.6	6.9	5.6	4.0	3.0	2.1	1.7	2.1	3.5	5.9	9.8	64.1

Part IV

The Caribbean and Bermuda
South America
Central America

CHAPTER 9

The Caribbean and Bermuda

Caribbean weather is tropical, warm, humid, and rainy. It is also beautiful and dramatic. Humidity is always high. Rain is more plentiful during the summer, particularly from August to October. The hurricane season runs from June through November, peaking in September. If you want to see the Caribbean at its best, late winter or early spring would be your best bet.

The climate of the Bahamas is tropical and much like South Florida. Temperatures are warm and the humidity high all year long. Rain falls primarily during June through October, peaking in September. The driest months are February and March. A late winter or early spring trip to Nassau would find the best weather conditions.

Bermuda, a small island in the Atlantic about 875 miles east of Charleston, South Carolina, has a pleasant climate. It's tropical in the summer and mild in the winter, and it rains quite a bit all year long. Summer humidity can be high. The best months to visit are April through June.

BAHAMAS

NASSAU — 12 ft.

	JAN	FEB	MAR	APR	MAY	JUN	JUL	AUG	SEP	OCT	NOV	DEC	ANN.
Av. High °F	77	77	79	81	84	87	88	89	88	85	81	79	83
Av. Low °F	65	64	66	69	71	74	75	76	75	73	70	67	70
Humidity	Hi	Hi	Hi	Hi	Hi	V.Hi	V.Hi	V.Hi	V.Hi	V.Hi	V.Hi	Hi	Hi
Precip. Days	6	5	5	6	9	12	14	14	15	13	9	6	114
Precip. In.	1.4	1.5	1.4	2.5	4.6	6.4	5.8	5.3	6.9	6.5	2.8	1.3	46.4

BARBADOS

BRIDGETOWN — 181 ft.

	JAN	FEB	MAR	APR	MAY	JUN	JUL	AUG	SEP	OCT	NOV	DEC	ANN.
Av. High °F	83	83	85	86	87	87	86	87	87	86	85	83	85
Av. Low °F	70	69	70	72	73	74	74	74	74	73	73	71	72
Humidity	Hi	Hi	Hi	Hi	Hi	Hi	V.Hi	V.Hi	V.Hi	V.Hi	V.Hi	Hi	Hi
Precip. Days	13	8	8	7	9	14	18	16	15	15	16	14	153
Precip. In.	2.6	1.1	1.3	1.4	2.3	4.4	5.8	5.8	6.7	7.0	8.1	3.8	50.2

BERMUDA

HAMILTON — 151 ft.

	JAN	FEB	MAR	APR	MAY	JUN	JUL	AUG	SEP	OCT	NOV	DEC	ANN.
Av. High °F	68	68	68	71	76	81	85	86	84	79	74	70	76
Av. Low °F	58	57	57	59	64	69	73	74	72	69	63	60	65
Humidity	Med	Med	Med	Med	Hi	Hi	V.Hi	V.Hi	V.Hi	Hi	Hi	Hi	Hi
Precip. Days	14	13	12	9	9	9	10	13	10	12	13	15	139
Precip. In.	4.4	4.7	4.8	4.1	4.6	4.4	4.5	5.4	5.2	5.8	5.0	4.7	57.6

JAMAICA

KINGSTON — 110 ft.

	JAN	FEB	MAR	APR	MAY	JUN	JUL	AUG	SEP	OCT	NOV	DEC	ANN.
Av. High °F	86	86	86	87	87	89	90	90	89	88	87	87	88
Av. Low °F	67	67	68	70	72	74	73	73	73	73	71	69	71
Humidity	Hi	Hi	Hi	Hi	V.Hi	V.Hi	V.Hi	V.Hi	V.Hi	V.Hi	V.Hi	Hi	V.Hi
Precip. Days	3	3	2	3	4	5	4	7	6	9	5	4	55
Precip. In.	.9	.6	.9	1.2	4.0	3.5	1.5	3.6	3.9	7.1	2.9	1.4	31.5

PUERTO RICO

S A N   J U A N — 82 ft.

	JAN	FEB	MAR	APR	MAY	JUN	JUL	AUG	SEP	OCT	NOV	DEC	ANN.
Av. High °F	80	80	81	82	84	85	85	85	86	85	84	81	83
Av. Low °F	70	70	70	72	74	75	75	76	75	75	73	72	73
Humidity	Hi	Hi	Hi	V.Hi	V.Hi	V.Hi	V.Hi	V.Hi	V.Hi	V.Hi	V.Hi	V.Hi	V.Hi
Precip. Days	20	15	15	14	16	17	19	20	18	18	19	21	212
Precip. In.	4.3	2.7	2.9	4.1	5.9	5.4	5.7	6.3	6.2	5.6	6.3	5.4	60.8

U.S. VIRGIN ISLANDS

S T.   T H O M A S — 11 ft.

	JAN	FEB	MAR	APR	MAY	JUN	JUL	AUG	SEP	OCT	NOV	DEC	ANN.
Av. High °F	82	83	84	85	86	87	88	88	88	87	86	84	86
Av. Low °F	71	71	72	74	75	77	77	77	76	76	74	73	74
Humidity	Hi	Hi	Hi	Hi	V.Hi	V.Hi	V.Hi	V.Hi	V.Hi	V.Hi	V.Hi	V.Hi	V.Hi
Precip. Days	9	7	6	8	10	9	10	12	14	13	10	10	118
Precip. In.	2.5	1.9	1.7	2.2	4.6	3.2	3.3	4.1	6.9	5.6	3.9	3.9	43.8

LOWEST GLOBAL SEA LEVEL PRESSURE: 25.69"
*520 miles northwest of Guam in the eye of
Typhoon "Tip" — October 12, 1979*

CHAPTER 10

South America

The most important thing to remember about the climate of South America is that its seasons are opposite those of the Northern Hemisphere—the warmest months occur during our winter, and the coolest temperatures happen during our summer. This presents a pleasant opportunity for those who like to get away from the cold and head for summer in January.

The primary South American travel destination is Rio. Its climate is subtropical, with warm, humid conditions prevailing the year round. There is no distinct rainy season, although the driest months are June through August. Even though this is their winter, daytime highs average in the mid-70s, and this may be the best bet for mild, dry conditions.

Buenos Aires is cooler than Rio, with temperatures that resemble California. Unlike the Golden State, however, rainfall is evenly spaced through the year and humidity is high from December through March. For a combination of moderate temperature and humidity the best months to visit would be October, November, and April.

La Paz, Bolivia sits at an elevation of 13,166 feet. This means that the air is thin, and temperatures low. The high temperatures average a consistent 55 to 59 degrees all year. Nights are cold with average lows ranging from 27 in the Southern Hemisphere winter to 39 degrees in January and February. Humidity is consistently low. The rainy season occurs during the warmer months, that is, December through February. The driest month is June. If you want the most sunshine, visit La Paz in June and July. If you want nights above freezing you'll have to visit during the rainier months. No matter when you visit, make sure you have a jacket and be prepared for the cold.

Santiago, Chile has a comfortable, pleasant climate with low humidity and rainfall. During the cooler months of June and July, highs average in the 50s with average rainfall of 3 inches each month. During the warmer months, highs reach the 80s, lows are in the 50s, and rainfall is rare. If this sounds a lot like Northern California, it is. Santiago is almost a mirror image of San Francisco Bay Area temperature and rainfall patterns. However, the seasons are reversed.

Bogotá, Colombia is another high elevation city. At 8,357 feet, it is consistently cool with highs in the 60s and lows in the 40s. Humidity is always comfortable. Rainfall can be frequent—almost daily during many months. The best time to visit would be December, January, or February. These months are the driest and sunniest.

Lima, Peru is a coastal city with the distinction of having an extreme desert climate—although a cool desert with plenty of fog. Daytime temperatures are comfortable through the year, ranging from the 60s in the coolest months to 80 in February. Nights are mild with lows in the upper 50s to upper 60s. The yearly rainfall averages only 1.6 inch. Rainfall is rare during December through April. The best time to visit would be during these mild, dry months.

Caracas, Venezuela sits at an elevation of 3,418 feet and is much cooler than its latitude (10° north) would imply. Temperatures are mild to warm all year, and humidity is moderate to high. Rainfall has a definite season and falls mostly from May through November. The best months to visit would be during the dry months of January through March. During February it rains on the average only two days, afternoon temperatures are in the upper 70s, and humidity is moderate—and that's hard to beat for an ideal time to visit.

ARGENTINA

BUENOS AIRES — 89 ft.

	JAN	FEB	MAR	APR	MAY	JUN	JUL	AUG	SEP	OCT	NOV	DEC	ANN.
Av. High °F	85	83	79	72	64	57	57	60	64	69	76	82	71
Av. Low °F	63	63	60	53	47	41	42	43	46	50	56	61	52
Humidity	Hi	Hi	Hi	Med	Med	Lo	Lo	Lo	Lo	Med	Med	Hi	Med
Precip. Days	7	6	7	8	7	7	8	9	8	9	9	8	93
Precip. In.	3.1	2.8	4.3	3.5	3.0	2.4	2.2	2.4	3.1	3.4	3.3	3.9	37.4

BOLIVIA

LA PAZ — 13,166 ft.

	JAN	FEB	MAR	APR	MAY	JUN	JUL	AUG	SEP	OCT	NOV	DEC	ANN.
Av. High °F	55	56	56	57	57	55	55	56	57	58	59	58	56
Av. Low °F	39	39	38	36	32	28	27	29	32	36	38	38	34
Humidity	V.Lo	V.Lo	V.Lo	V.Lo	V.Lo	V.Lo	V.Lo	V.Lo	V.Lo	V.Lo	V.Lo	V.Lo	V.Lo
Precip. Days	22	16	14	9	4	3	3	6	8	10	12	16	123
Precip. In.	4.5	4.2	2.6	1.3	.5	.3	.4	.5	1.1	1.6	1.9	3.7	22.6

BRAZIL

RIO DE JANEIRO — 201 ft.

	JAN	FEB	MAR	APR	MAY	JUN	JUL	AUG	SEP	OCT	NOV	DEC	ANN.
Av. High °F	84	85	83	80	77	76	75	76	75	77	79	82	79
Av. Low °F	73	73	72	69	66	64	63	64	65	66	68	71	68
Humidity	Hi	V.Hi	V.Hi	Hi	Hi	Hi	Hi	Hi	Hi	Hi	Hi	Hi	Hi
Precip. Days	13	11	12	10	10	7	7	7	11	13	13	14	128
Precip. In.	4.9	4.8	5.1	4.2	3.1	2.1	1.6	1.7	2.6	3.1	4.1	5.4	42.6

CHILE

SANTIAGO — 1,555 ft.

	JAN	FEB	MAR	APR	MAY	JUN	JUL	AUG	SEP	OCT	NOV	DEC	ANN.
Av. High °F	85	84	80	72	64	58	57	61	65	71	77	82	71
Av. Low °F	54	53	49	45	41	38	37	39	42	45	48	51	45
Humidity	Med	Med	Med	Lo	Lo	Lo	Lo	Lo	Lo	Lo	Lo	Med	Lo
Precip. Days	1	1	2	4	7	7	9	7	6	4	3	1	52
Precip. In.	.1	.1	.2	.5	2.5	3.3	3.0	2.2	1.2	.6	.3	.2	14.1

COLOMBIA

B O G O T A — 8,357 ft.

	JAN	FEB	MAR	APR	MAY	JUN	JUL	AUG	SEP	OCT	NOV	DEC	ANN.
Av. High °F	66	66	67	66	65	64	64	64	65	65	65	66	65
Av. Low °F	43	45	47	48	48	48	47	46	46	47	47	45	46
Humidity	Lo	Lo	Med	Med	Med	Med	Lo	Lo	Lo	Med	Med	Lo	Lo
Precip. Days	10	12	16	21	23	21	20	20	20	21	18	14	216
Precip. In.	2.3	2.6	4.0	5.8	4.4	2.4	2.0	2.2	2.4	6.3	4.7	2.6	41.7

PERU

L I M A — 43 ft.

	JAN	FEB	MAR	APR	MAY	JUN	JUL	AUG	SEP	OCT	NOV	DEC	ANN.
Av. High °F	79	80	80	76	72	69	67	66	68	69	72	76	73
Av. Low °F	68	69	69	66	63	61	60	60	59	61	63	66	64
Humidity	Hi	Hi	Hi	Hi	Hi	Med	Med	Med	Med	Med	Hi	Hi	Hi
Precip. Days	3	2	3	2	7	12	14	18	16	10	5	4	96
Precip. In.	.1	T	T	T	.2	.2	.3	.3	.3	.1	.1	T	1.6

VENEZUELA

C A R A C A S — 3,418 ft.

	JAN	FEB	MAR	APR	MAY	JUN	JUL	AUG	SEP	OCT	NOV	DEC	ANN.
Av. High °F	75	77	79	81	80	78	78	79	80	79	77	78	78
Av. Low °F	56	56	58	60	62	62	61	61	61	61	60	58	60
Humidity	Med	Med	Med	Hi	Hi	Hi	Hi	Hi	Hi	Hi	Hi	Med	Hi
Precip. Days	6	2	3	4	9	14	15	15	13	12	13	10	116
Precip. In.	.9	.4	.6	1.3	3.1	4.0	4.3	4.3	4.2	4.3	3.7	1.8	32.8

LOWEST GLOBAL AVERAGE ANNUAL RAINFALL: 0.03"
Arica, Chile

CHAPTER 11

Central America

Much of Central America is mountainous and covered with lush rain forests. The primary cities are in the interior, several thousand feet above sea level, where temperatures are mild all year long. The driest months are December through March. In San José, Costa Rica, and much of interior Central America, the driest and least humid month is February.

Coastal cities near sea level are consistently warm and humid. Highs average in the 80s or low 90s. Lows are in the upper 60s to upper 70s. Humidity is consistently high or very high.

However, any location facing toward the Caribbean will experience consistently moderate or high rainfall through the year. Locations facing the Pacific enjoy a distinct dry season lasting from December through April.

Many larger cities enjoy a wonderful climate since they are located at higher elevations where temperatures are cooler. For example, Guatemala City, at 4,917 feet, enjoys all-year highs in the 70s with lows in the 50s and 60s. The best time to visit would be December through March when rainfall is low and sunshine high.

Other interior cities at high elevations experience similar relief from daily rainfall during the winter months. All Central American cities have frequent and heavy rainfall during the summer months.

BELIZE

BELIZE — 16 ft.

	JAN	FEB	MAR	APR	MAY	JUN	JUL	AUG	SEP	OCT	NOV	DEC	ANN.
Av. High °F	81	82	84	86	87	87	87	88	87	86	83	81	85
Av. Low °F	67	68	71	74	75	75	75	75	74	72	68	68	72
Humidity	V.Hi	V.Hi	V.Hi	X.Hi	V.Hi	X.Hi	X.Hi	V.Hi	X.Hi	V.Hi	V.Hi	V.Hi	V.Hi
Precip. Days	24	6	4	6	9	15	13	13	14	19	16	29	169
Precip. In.	6.6	2.8	1.8	2.8	5.8	9.8	7.7	7.8	9.2	13.2	10.5	7.7	85.7

COSTA RICA

SAN JOSÉ — 3,760 ft.

	JAN	FEB	MAR	APR	MAY	JUN	JUL	AUG	SEP	OCT	NOV	DEC	ANN.
Av. High °F	75	76	79	79	80	79	77	78	79	77	77	75	77
Av. Low °F	58	58	59	62	62	62	62	61	61	60	60	58	60
Humidity	Med	Med	Med	Hi	Hi	Hi	Hi	Hi	Hi	Hi	Hi	Hi	Hi
Precip. Days	3	1	2	7	19	22	23	24	24	25	14	6	170
Precip. In.	.6	.2	.8	1.8	9.0	9.5	8.3	9.5	12.0	11.8	5.7	1.6	70.8

EL SALVADOR

SAN SALVADOR — 2,037 ft.

	JAN	FEB	MAR	APR	MAY	JUN	JUL	AUG	SEP	OCT	NOV	DEC	ANN.
Av. High °F	83	85	86	87	84	82	83	83	81	82	82	82	83
Av. Low °F	65	66	67	70	70	70	69	69	69	68	65	66	68
Humidity	Hi	Hi	Hi	Hi	Hi	Hi	Hi	Hi	Hi	Hi	Hi	Hi	Hi
Precip. Days	2	1	3	5	11	17	15	19	20	14	5	2	114
Precip. In.	.3	.2	.4	1.7	7.7	12.9	11.5	11.7	12.1	9.5	1.6	.4	70.0

GUATEMALA

GUATEMALA CITY — 4,917 ft.

	JAN	FEB	MAR	APR	MAY	JUN	JUL	AUG	SEP	OCT	NOV	DEC	ANN.
Av. High °F	72	75	77	78	78	75	74	74	73	73	72	72	74
Av. Low °F	55	56	58	60	62	62	61	61	61	61	58	57	59
Humidity	Med	Med	Med	Med	Med	Hi	Med	Hi	Hi	Med	Med	Med	Med
Precip. Days	4	3	4	5	14	23	20	20	23	15	7	5	143
Precip. In.	.3	.1	.5	1.2	6.0	10.8	8.0	7.8	9.1	6.8	.9	.3	51.8

HONDURAS

TEGUCIGALPA — 3,260 ft.

	JAN	FEB	MAR	APR	MAY	JUN	JUL	AUG	SEP	OCT	NOV	DEC	ANN.
Av. High °F	77	80	84	85	85	82	81	82	82	80	78	76	81
Av. Low °F	59	60	62	62	66	66	65	65	65	64	62	61	63
Humidity	Med	Med	Med	Med	Hi	Hi	Hi	Hi	Hi	Hi	Hi	Med	Hi
Precip. Days	5	3	2	2	9	13	11	11	16	13	8	7	100
Precip. In.	.5	.1	0	1.0	7.1	7.0	2.8	2.9	5.9	3.4	1.5	.5	32.7

NICARAGUA

MANAGUA — 164 ft.

	JAN	FEB	MAR	APR	MAY	JUN	JUL	AUG	SEP	OCT	NOV	DEC	ANN.
Av. High °F	88	90	92	93	92	88	87	88	87	87	88	87	89
Av. Low °F	70	71	73	75	76	75	74	74	74	73	72	71	73
Humidity	Hi	Hi	Hi	Hi	V.Hi	V.Hi	V.Hi	V.Hi	V.Hi	V.Hi	V.Hi	Hi	V.Hi
Precip. Days	3	1	1	1	6	21	20	17	20	19	10	2	121
Precip. In.	.2	0	.2	.2	3.0	11.7	5.3	5.1	7.2	9.6	2.3	.2	45.0

PANAMA

PANAMA CITY (Balboa Heights) — 118 ft.

	JAN	FEB	MAR	APR	MAY	JUN	JUL	AUG	SEP	OCT	NOV	DEC	ANN.
Av. High °F	88	89	90	87	86	87	87	86	85	85	85	87	87
Av. Low °F	71	71	72	74	74	74	74	74	74	73	73	73	73
Humidity	V.Hi	V.Hi	V.Hi	V.Hi	V.Hi	V.Hi	V.Hi	V.Hi	V.Hi	V.Hi	V.Hi	V.Hi	V.Hi
Precip. Days	4	2	1	6	15	16	15	15	16	18	18	12	137
Precip. In.	1.0	.4	.7	2.9	8.0	8.4	7.1	7.9	8.2	10.1	10.2	4.8	69.7

Index

A

Acapulco, Mexico, 57-58
Adelaide, Australia, 98
Africa, 80-82
Alabama, 40
Alaska, 21-22
Albany, New York, 26
Albuquerque, New Mexico, 51
Alice Springs, Australia, 98
Amsterdam, The Netherlands, 68
Anchorage, Alaska, 21-22
Argentina, 108, 110
Arizona, 47
Arkansas, 40
Asia, 89-96
Aspen, Colorado, 50
Athens, Greece, 71-72
Atlanta, Georgia, 42
Atlantic City, New Jersey, 26
Auckland, New Zealand, 100-101
Austin, Texas, 44
Australia, 97-99
Austria, 65-66

B

Bahamas, 105-106
Bali, Indonesia, 92-93
Baltimore, Maryland, 25
Bangkok, Thailand, 92, 94
Barbados, 106
Barcelona, Spain, 78
Beijing, China, 89-90
Belfast, Northern Ireland, 64
Belgium, 65-66
Belize, 113
Bergen, Norway, 77
Berlin, Germany, 67
Bermuda, 105-6
Birmingham, Alabama, 40
Bismarck, North Dakota, 36
Bogotá, Colombia, 109, 111
Boise, Idaho, 50
Bolivia, 108-110
Bombay, India, 96

Bosnia and Herzegovina, 69
Boston, Massachusetts, 25
Brazil, 108-110
Bridgetown, Barbados, 106
Brisbane, Australia, 97-98
British Isles, 63-64
Brussels, Belgium, 66
Budapest, Hungary, 70
Buenos Aires, Argentina, 108-110
Buffalo, New York, 27
Burlington, Vermont, 28

C

Cairo, Egypt, 81
Calcutta, India, 96
Calgary, Canada, 55
California, 46, 48-49
Canada, 54-56
Cancun, Mexico, 58
Capetown, South Africa, 82
Caracas, Venezuela, 109, 111
Caribbean, 105-107
Casablanca, Morocco, 80-81
Cedar City, Utah, 52
Central America, 112-114
Central Europe, 65-68
Charleston, South Carolina, 43
Charleston, West Virginia, 45
Charlotte, North Carolina, 43
Chicago, Illinois, 33
Chile, 109-110
China, 89-90
Christchurch, New Zealand, 100-101
Cincinnati, Ohio, 36
Cleveland, Ohio, 36
Colombia, 109-111
Colorado, 50
Columbus, Ohio, 37
Concord, New Hampshire, 26
Connecticut, 24
Copenhagen, Denmark, 77
Costa Rica, 112-113
Cozumel, Mexico, 58
Czech Republic, 65, 70

More Travel Books from Ten Speed Press

The Packing Book (Revised)
by Judith Gilford

With 45,000 copies in print, this book is fast becoming a travel classic. Now, a revised edition covers innovations in luggage and offers more extensive packing tips for all kinds of trips.

Travel Journal

Quotes from famous travelers, journal pages, conversion charts, maps, U.S. and Canadian embassies, and more. Encased in a sturdy clear plastic jacket.

Everywoman's Travel Journal

Includes journal pages, health and safety tips, conversion charts for measurements and clothing sizes, special resources for women, and quotes from female travelers throughout history. Encased in a sturdy clear plastic jacket.

The Wordless Travel Book
by Jonathan Meader

This inventive little book enables you to communicate in any country just by pointing at its clear, colorful icons. You no longer need to speak to be understood!

For more information, or to order, call the publisher at the number below. We accept VISA, MasterCard, and American Express. You may also wish to write for our free catalog of over 500 books, posters, and audiotapes.

Ten Speed Press
P.O. Box 7123
Berkeley, CA 94707
(800) 841-BOOK

PRINTED IN CANADA